LawExpress

FAMILY LAW

Develop your legal skills

9781408226100

9781447905141

9781408261538

9781447922650

Written to help you develop the essential skills needed to succeed on your course and prepare for practice.

Available from all good bookshops or order online at:
www.pearsoned.co.uk/law

FAMILY LAW

Law Express

5th edition

Jonathan Herring
Exeter College, University of Oxford

Harlow, England • London • New York • Boston • San Francisco • Toronto • Sydney • Auckland • Singapore • Hong Kong
Tokyo • Seoul • Taipei • New Delhi • Cape Town • São Paulo • Mexico City • Madrid • Amsterdam • Munich • Paris • Milan

Pearson Education Limited
Edinburgh Gate
Harlow CM20 2JE
United Kingdom
Tel: +44 (0)1279 623623
Web: www.pearson.com/uk

First published 2007 (print)
Second edition published 2009 (print)
Third edition published 2011 (print)
Fourth edition published 2013 (print and
Fifth edition published 2015 (print and

© Pearson Education Limited 2007, 201
© Pearson Education Limited 2013, 201

The right of Jonathan Herring to be identi
with the Copyright, Designs and Patents A

Contains public sector information licensed under the Open Government Licence (OGL) v2.0.
www.nationalarchives.gov.uk/doc/open-government-licence.

Pearson Education is not responsible for the content of third-party internet sites.

ISBN: 978-1-292-01287-2 (print)
      978-1-292-01343-5 (PDF)
      978-1-292-01809-6 (ePub)
      978-1-292-01305-3 (eText)

British Library Cataloguing-in-Publication Data
A catalogue record for the print edition is available from the British Library

Library of Congress Cataloging-in-Publication Data
Herring, Jonathan, author.
    Family law / Jonathan Herring, Exeter College, University of Oxford. -- 5th edition.
        pages cm. – (Law express)
    Includes index.
    ISBN 978-1-292-01287-2 (pbk.) -- ISBN 9781292013435 (PDF) -- ISBN 978-1-292-01305-3 (eText)
1. Domestic relations--England--Outlines, syllabi, etc.   I. Title.
KD750.H4725 2015
346.4201'5--dc23
                                                                            2014001950
ARP impression 98

Print edition typeset in 10/12pt Helvetica Neue LT Std by 35
Print edition printed and bound in Great Britain by Ashford Colour Press Ltd

NOTE THAT ANY PAGE CROSS REFERENCES REFER TO THE PRINT EDITION

Contents

Supporting resources

Visit the *Law Express* series companion website at **www.pearsoned.co.uk/ lawexpress** to find valuable student learning material including:

- A **study plan** test to help you assess how well you know the subject before you begin your revision
- Interactive **quizzes** to test your knowledge of the main points from each chapter
- Sample **examination questions** and guidelines for answering them
- Interactive **flashcards** to help you revise key terms, cases and statutes
- Printable versions of the **topic maps** and **checklists** from the book
- **'You be the marker'** allows you to see exam questions and answers from the perspective of the examiner and includes notes on how an answer might be marked
- **Podcasts** provide point-by-point instruction on how to answer a typical exam question

Also: The companion website provides the following features:

- Search tool to help locate specific items of content
- E-mail results and profile tools to send results of quizzes to instructors
- Online help and support to assist with website usage and troubleshooting

For more information please contact your local Pearson Education sales representative or visit **www.pearsoned.co.uk/lawexpress**

Acknowledgements

I am very grateful to those who reviewed a sample chapter of this book and provided some very useful comments. Laura Blake, Donna Goddard and Christine Statham at Pearson Education have been extremely helpful with guidance on the format and flavour of the series. Above all, I am grateful to Kirsten, Laurel, Jo and Darcy who were loving and supportive beyond measure during the writing of the book.

Jonathan Herring
Exeter College, University of Oxford

Publisher's acknowledgements

Our thanks go to all reviewers who contributed to the development of this text, including students who participated in research and focus groups which helped to shape the series format.

Introduction

Family law is a very popular option at most universities. It is about the very stuff of life: love, care, relationships, sex. The facts of the cases are easy to understand. Certainly more so than those dreadful contract law cases involving stevedores! But there is a danger that in studying family law you get so carried away with the stories that you forget to state the law. Some students get so excited with, for example, writing about the injustices faced by unmarried fathers in family law that they forget to mention any law at all. So family law is meant to be an enjoyable subject and, understandably, you will have strong views on the issues raised. However, in the exam room, control yourself. Make sure you persuade the examiner that you know the key legal principles, the important statutory provisions and the leading cases. That said, a family law essay that is no more than a recital of cases or statutory provisions will score low marks – and bore the examiner, which is never advisable.

This book is divided up into 10 chapters and your course is likely to have been divided up into sections something like this. However, do not let this restrict your thinking. In family law, these topics interact. The law on divorce impacts on the law on marriage. Our definition of a parent affects what obligations parents owe their children. So, even if an essay is asking you about one topic, always think about how similar issues are raised in other topics. There are some theoretical issues that run throughout family law. Should we focus on *form* (e.g. whether the couple are married; whether a person is in law a father or mother) or *reality* (e.g. what is their relationship like? What are they doing with their child?)? Should the courts be given discretion in order to reach results that are fair, or should they apply rules so that the law can be more predictable? Does family law continue to work against the interests of women or has the tide turned so that it now works against the interests of men?

This book is designed to help you focus as you revise for your examinations. It is in no way a replacement for attending lectures or reading the leading cases, articles and textbooks. A top-rated answer is likely to include references to more cases than are found here and will raise more theoretical issues than are mentioned. What this book can do is to set you off on a good sound footing for your revision. It will outline the most important points that you *must* know. It also provides you with some pointers as to how to move on by providing you with ideas to think about and some reading to look at. Hopefully, quite a bit of what you will find here you will already have come across, but this will provide you with a sound overview. The book should set your mind at rest: you *do* know the basics and you now have the tools to excel in your exams.

📖 **REVISION NOTE**

- Don't get too carried away with your arguments. You must persuade the examiner that you know the law.
- Show the examiner that you can see how the topics interrelate. Don't treat the subject as a set of discrete boxes.
- In problem questions, be practical. Always consider the range of orders the court might employ, but remember: they have to be enforced and workable.

Before you begin, you can use the study plan available on the companion website to assess how well you know the material in this book and identify the areas where you may want to focus your revision.

Guided tour

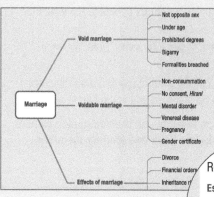

Marriage
- Void marriage
  - Not opposite sex
  - Under age
  - Prohibited degrees
  - Bigamy
  - Formalities breached
- Voidable marriage
  - Non-consummation
  - No consent, *Hirani*
  - Mental disorder
  - Venereal disease
  - Pregnancy
  - Gender certificate
- Effects of marriage
  - Divorce
  - Financial orders
  - Inheritance r...

Topic maps – Visual guides highlight key subject areas and facilitate easy navigation through the chapter. Download them from the companion website to pin on your wall or add to your revision notes.

Revision checklists – How well do you know each topic? Use these to identify essential points you should know for your exams. But don't panic if you don't know them all – the chapters will help you revise each point to ensure you are fully prepared. Print the checklists off the companion website and track your revision progress!

Revision checklist

Essential points you shoul

- [ ] The meaning and use of the
- [ ] How the Human Rights Act i
- [ ] The checklist of factors
- [ ] The law on residence ap

Sample questions with answer guidelines – Practice makes perfect! Read the question at the start of each chapter and consider how you would answer it. Guidance on structuring strong answers is provided at the end of the chapter. Try out additional sample questions online.

▓ Sample question

Could you answer this question? Below is a typical essay question that could arise on this topic. Guidelines on answering the question are included at the end of this chapter; a sample problem question and guidance on tackling it can be found on the companion website.

Assessment advice – Not sure how best to tackle a problem or essay question? Wondering what you may be asked? Use the assessment advice to identify the ways in which a subject may be examined and how to apply your knowledge effectively.

ASSESSMENT ADVICE

Essay questions

Essays on child protection often centre around the interpretation of the threshold criteria in section 31, Children Act 1989, which set out the circumstances in which a care or supervision order is made. The cases interpreting these can be seen as requiring a delicate balance between protecting the interests of the parents in having their children removed improperly and protecting children from abuse by ensuring that if they are in danger they can be protected. This is an area where the Human Rights Act has played a significant role and so it is useful to bring into an essay a discussion of how a human rights approach could be applied in this area.

Key definitions – Make sure you understand essential legal terms. Use the flashcards online to test your recall!

KEY DEFINITION: Placement

This is where the child lives with the would-be adopters as a form of 'trial' period to see if the adoption is likely to work. Note that a child can only be placed if the 'placement conditions' are met, which most importantly require the parents to have consented to the making of the adoption order or for their consent to have been dispensed with.

Key cases and key statutes
– Identify and review the important elements of the essential cases and statutes you will need to know for your exams.

KEY STATUTE

Family Law Act 1996
In deciding whether or to all the circumstance

(a) of the applicant [,
(b) of any relevant

KEY CASE

C v C (Non-Molestation Order: Jurisdiction) [1998] 1 FCR 11 (HC)
Concerning: the meaning of molestation

Facts
The wife had communicated with journalists about her relationship with her husband. He sought a non-molestation order to prevent her from making revelations in newspapers about their life together.

Make your answer stand out – This
feature illustrates sources of further thinking and debate where you can maximise your marks. Use them to really impress your examiners!

✓ Make your answer stand out

Remember that *Radmacher* does not say that pre-nups will always be enforceable. A party can claim that the pre-nup was not properly entered into (e.g. there was not full disclosure; there was undue pressure); or that the agreement was unfair (e.g. it did not adequately provide for the children of the marriage). However a pre-nup can certainly be upheld, even if it gives a wife significantly less than half the assets (*Z* v *Z* (2011)).

Be aware of some of the academic commentary on the decision. Contrast George *et al.* (2011) who oppose the decision and Miles (2011) who is more sympathetic.

Exam tips – Feeling the pressure? These
boxes indicate how you can improve your exam performance when it really counts.

✎ EXAM TIP

We have highlighted here in brief some of the major differences in the grounds for making the occupation orders under each section and the kinds of orders that can be made. An excellent candidate will be aware of all of the differences between the sections.

Revision notes – Get guidance for effective
revision. These boxes highlight related points and areas of overlap in the subject, or areas where your course might adopt a particular approach that you should check with your course tutor.

⬚ REVISION NOTE

When thinking about the weight the court should give and does give to children's wishes in these cases, tie this in with the discussion about children's rights in Chapter 8.

Don't be tempted to ... – This feature
underlines areas where students most often trip up in exams. Use them to spot common pitfalls and avoid losing marks.

❗ Don't be tempted to . . .

Don't assume that if the threshold criteria are met the court must make a care order. The threshold criteria permit, but do not require, the court to make a care or supervision order. In *Re B (Children)* (2012) even though the children were at risk of suffering significant harm the court determined it was better not to make a care order but instead help the parents be better parents.

Read to impress – Focus on these carefully
selected sources to extend your knowledge, deepen your understanding, and earn better marks in coursework as well as in exams.

READ TO IMPRESS

Bainham, A. (2006) The Rights and Obligations Associated with the Birth of a Child, in Spencer, J. and du Bois-Pedain, A. (eds) *Freedom and Responsibility in Reproductive Choice.* Oxford: Hart.

Bainham, A. (2008) Arguments over Parentage, 67 *Cambridge Law Journal* 322.

Diduck, A. (2007) If only we can Find the Appropriate Terms to Use the Issue will be Solved: Law, Identity and Parenthood, *Child and Family Law Quarterly* 458.

Glossary – Forgotten the meaning of a
word? This quick reference covers key definitions and other useful terms.

Glossary of terms

The glossary is divided into two parts: key definitions and other useful terms. The key definitions can be found within the chapter in which they occur as well as in the glossary below. These definitions are the essential terms that you must know and understand in order to prepare for an exam. The additional list of terms provides further definitions of

Guided tour of the companion website

 Book resources are available to download. Print your own **topic maps** and **revision checklists**!

 Use the **study plan** prior to your revision to help you assess how well you know the subject and determine which areas need most attention. Choose to take the full assessment or focus on targeted study units.

 'Test your knowledge' of individual areas with quizzes tailored specifically to each chapter. **Sample problem and essay questions** are also available with guidance on writing a good answer.

 Flashcards test and improve recall of important legal terms, key cases and statutes. Available in both electronic and printable formats.

'You be the marker' gives you the chance to evaluate sample exam answers for different question types and understand how and why an examiner awards marks.

Download the **podcast** and listen as your own personal Law Express tutor guides you through answering a typical but challenging question. A step-by-step explanation on how to approach the question is provided, including what essential elements your answer will need for a pass, how to structure a good response, and what to do to make your answer stand out so that you can earn extra marks.

All of this and more can be found when you visit **www.pearsoned.co.uk/lawexpress**

Table of cases and statutes

■ Cases

■ Statutes

■ Statutory instruments

■ International treaties and conventions

Marriage and civil partnership

Revision checklist

Essential points you should know:

- [ ] The grounds on which a marriage or civil partnership can be void
- [ ] The grounds on which a marriage or civil partnership can be voidable
- [ ] The differences between marriage and civil partnership
- [ ] The debates surrounding whether same-sex couples should be permitted to marry

◼ Topic map

```
                                              ┌─── Not opposite sex
                                              │
                                              ├─── Under age
                                              │
                        Void marriage ────────┼─── Prohibited degrees
                                              │
                                              ├─── Bigamy
                                              │
                                              └─── Formalities breached


                                              ┌─── Non-consummation
                                              │
                                              ├─── No consent, Hirani
                                              │
    ┌──────────┐                              ├─── Mental disorder
    │ Marriage │──────── Voidable marriage ───┤
    └──────────┘                              ├─── Venereal disease
                                              │
                                              ├─── Pregnancy
                                              │
                                              └─── Gender certificate


                                              ┌─── Divorce
                                              │
                                              ├─── Financial orders
                                              │
                      Effects of marriage ────┼─── Inheritance rights
                                              │
                                              ├─── Parental responsibility
                                              │
                                              └─── Tax advantages
```

A printable version of this topic map is available from **www.pearsoned.co.uk/lawexpress**

■ Introduction

Before giving advice to a couple on a family law issue, it is essential to know whether or not they are married or civil partners.

This chapter will look at the age-old institution of marriage and the relatively new status of civil partnership. Over the years the legal significance of marriage has decreased. There is now an impressive array of statutes that give married and unmarried couples the same rights (e.g. Rent Act 1977, Family Law Act 1996). Nevertheless, marriage and civil partnership do carry some important legal rights and responsibilities. But perhaps more important than that, they provide a degree of social respect and acknowledgement of the relationship. Therefore, the laws on which couples can or cannot marry or enter civil partnerships tell us something about which kinds of relationship our legal system values. The Marriage (Same-Sex Couples) Act 2013 will allow same-sex couples the opportunity to marry, making a clear break from the traditionally religious origins of marriage.

ASSESSMENT ADVICE

Essay questions

There are two favourite areas for essay questions on this topic. The first is the issue of which couples can or cannot marry (or enter a civil partnership). You need to be able to explain the restrictions on marriage and discuss whether they are justifiable. The second is a question asking about the legal consequences of marriage or civil partnership. You need to be able to explain these, and particularly how marriage and civil partnership differ.

Problem questions

Problem questions often focus on the issues surrounding void and voidable marriages and civil partnerships. You will need to have a detailed knowledge of the case law. Students often do not know enough about the bars to relief (which is understandable because it is a rather boring area of the law!).

■ Sample question

Could you answer this question? Below is a typical essay question that could arise on this topic. Guidelines on answering the question are included at the end of this chapter; a sample problem question and guidance on tackling it can be found on the companion website.

> ### ESSAY QUESTION
>
> Discuss the differences between civil partnerships and marriages. Should the law have been changed to allowed same-sex couple to marry?

■ Who can marry whom?

The Matrimonial Causes Act 1973, section 11 sets out which marriages are void:

- marriages between people within the **prohibited degrees of relationship** (e.g. a brother and a sister);
- either of the parties is under 16;
- either of the parties is married to someone else. If they were previously married but the marriage has ended through death or divorce, they are free to marry.

The Marriage (Same-Sex Couples) Act 2013 has removed the provision that used to prevent same-sex couples marrying.

As long as the couple are not within one of these categories, they are free to enter a valid marriage. You will need to make sure you have learned this list of void marriages for the exam. Most of these requirements are straightforward. But there are some issues we need to look at in more detail.

Same-sex marriage

Gay marriage is now possible, but perhaps oddly, there are a few differences between same-sex marriage and opposite-sex marriage. The most striking differences are:

- A same-sex marriage cannot be voidable if there is a lack of **consummation**. An opposite-sex marriage can be (see pages 7–8)
- A same-sex couple cannot rely on same-sex **adultery** as the basis for a divorce petition, an opposite-sex couple can (see Chapter 4).

This means it is still necessary to determine the sex of the parties to marriage to know which set of rules apply.

KEY DEFINITION: Male and female

The definition of male is that at birth the individual's genital, gonadal and chromosomal characteristics all pointed in the direction of being male. The equivalent is true for female. Psychological factors are not taken into account. If someone's biological factors at birth are mixed, a court can also consider other factors, including psychological factors that materialise later in life. The Gender Recognition Act 2004 enables someone to apply for a Gender Recognition Certificate, which recognises for legal purposes that their sex is that in which they now live.

✎ EXAM TIP

A question that is interesting to discuss in an essay is why sex is defined in terms of biological rather than psychological factors. Should what is between the legs matter more than what is in the head? Some people have even argued that we should reject the idea that everyone is either male or female and instead recognise a sexual scale with people at different points on it (see Chau and Herring (2002)).

The Gender Recognition Act 2004

This Act enables someone to apply for a **Gender Recognition Certificate** so that his or her legal sex will be the '**acquired gender**' (i.e. the gender the person wishes to be recognised as having).

KEY STATUTE

Gender Recognition Act 2004, section 2(1)

1 '. . . the [Gender Recognition] Panel must grant the application if satisfied that the applicant –

(a) has or has had gender dysphoria;

(b) has lived in the acquired gender throughout the period of two years ending with the date on which the application is made;

(c) intends to continue to live in the acquired gender until death; and

(d) complies with the requirements [for producing medical reports and other supporting evidence] imposed by and under section 3.'

Once a Gender Recognition Certificate is issued, the person's acquired gender is his or her gender for all purposes (Gender Recognition Act 2004, section 9). Note that it is not necessary for a person to have received surgery in order to obtain a certificate.

Marrying for bad reasons

The law does not enquire as to why people are marrying. There is no legal requirement for them to be in love, for example! In New Zealand the courts upheld the marriage of two students who got married simply so that they could get better student grants and loans. As the following case illustrates, the English and Welsh courts will be unwilling to bar people legally entitled to marry from doing so because they are acting from questionable motives!

KEY CASE

R (on the application of the CPS) v *Registrar General* [2003] QB 1222 (CA)

Concerning: whether the state could stop people marrying for improper purposes

Facts

A man was facing trial for murder. He and the woman who was to be the chief prosecution witness sought to marry. Under the law of evidence, a wife cannot be compelled to give evidence against her husband (except in certain unusual circumstances). The Crown Prosecution Service sought an order that the Registrar General of Births, Marriages and Deaths should not issue a marriage certificate on the ground of public policy.

Legal principle

It was held that the Registrar General did not have the power to stop two people from marrying on the ground of public policy. The Human Rights Act 1998 protected the right to marry and that did not depend on a person having a good reason for marrying.

■ Voidable marriages

The differences between a void marriage and a voidable marriage

It is important to distinguish a marriage that is voidable from a marriage that is void. If you are answering a problem question in the exam, make sure that it is clear whether you are discussing a void or voidable marriage. You may also need to explain the differences in the consequences of a marriage being found to be void or voidable. The key differences are as follows.

Void marriage	Voidable marriage
The marriage is automatically void; there is no need to obtain a court order to say so	The marriage can only be set aside if there is a court order. Without a court order annulling the marriage, it is a valid one
Any person can apply to have a marriage declared void	Only the parties to the marriage can apply to have a voidable marriage annulled
A child born to a couple in a void marriage is 'illegitimate' unless the couple believed their marriage to be valid. However, illegitimacy has very little significance in law today	A child born to a couple in a voidable marriage is not 'illegitimate'

✎ EXAM TIP

A useful point to make in exams is that, as well as these technical differences, the different grounds on which a marriage is void or voidable tell us something about the nature of marriage itself. The grounds on which a marriage is void tell us that there are public policy objections to the marriage, e.g. where one of the couple is under 16. In the case of voidable marriages, there is no public policy objection to the marriage, but there is a major flaw that, if it bothers either of the parties, should entitle them to have the marriage annulled, e.g. non-consummation. If, therefore, you are asked about what the law thinks is important about marriage, making this point is a useful way of starting your essay.

Grounds on which a marriage may be voidable

KEY STATUTE

Matrimonial Causes Act 1973, section 12

'A marriage celebrated after 31 July 1971 shall be voidable on the following grounds only, that is to say –

(a) that the marriage has not been consummated owing to the incapacity of either party to consummate it;

(b) that the marriage has not been consummated owing to the wilful refusal of the respondent to consummate it;

(c) that either party to the marriage did not validly consent to it, whether in consequence of duress, mistake, unsoundness of mind or otherwise; ▶

(d) that at the time of the marriage either party, though capable of giving a valid consent, was suffering (whether continuously or intermittently) from mental disorder within the meaning of the Mental Health Act 1983 of such a kind or to such an extent as to be unfitted for marriage;

(e) that at the time of the marriage the respondent was suffering from venereal disease in a communicable form;

(f) that at the time of the marriage the respondent was pregnant by some person other than the petitioner;

(g) that an Interim Gender Recognition Certificate under the Gender Recognition Act 2004

(h) that the respondent is a person whose gender at the time of the marriage has become the acquired gender under the Gender Recognition Act 2004.'

It may be that you are given a statute book in your exam and so will simply need to know which statute to look up to find this list of voidable grounds. If you are not, then you will need to learn this list. Many of these are self-explanatory. We shall focus on the less straightforward statutes.

Non-consummation

KEY DEFINITION: Consummation

Consummation is vaginal intercourse. The fact that contraception is used does not prevent there being consummation, but there must be penile penetration.

Notice that for an opposite-sex marriage to be annulled it is not enough just to show that the marriage has not been consummated. It must be shown that this is due to the incapacity of either party or the wilful refusal of the respondent. You cannot rely on your own wilful refusal to consummate in order to annul a marriage!

❗ Don't be tempted to . . .

Inability to consummate after marriage
A popular scenario in a problem question is where one of the parties to the marriage becomes physically unable to consummate the marriage after the marriage ceremony, but before there has been consummation. One of them suffers a serious car accident leaving the wedding reception, for example. Section 12 of the Matrimonial Causes Act does not make it clear when the inability must arise. The traditional church doctrine requires the voidable ground to be present at the time of the marriage. However, it may be that the policy behind allowing this voidable ground applies equally to a case where the inability arises before or after the marriage.

Lack of consent

A marriage is voidable if either party did not validly consent to it. The statute lists the kinds of factors that mean that a party did not consent: **duress**, mistake or unsound mind. Notice that the mistake must be a fundamental one, such as mistaken identity. It could not include a mistake that you thought your spouse was rich or a good lover, but he or she was not!

✎ EXAM TIP

Students can be mistaken over the 'lack of consent' ground. Following *Hirani* v *Hirani* (1982) and *NS* v *MI* (2006) the court will consider the effect of the threat, rather than the kind of threat. So it is not necessary to show that there was a threat of violence, only that the threat (whatever it was) had such an impact on the victim that she cannot be taken to have consented to the marriage. Note, however, that the courts recognise that there is no objection to an arranged marriage. Even if there is family pressure on a person to marry, the marriage will not be invalid, unless there are very powerful threats.

Forced marriage

There have been quite a few cases in recent years that have involved forced marriages (see e.g. *P* v *R* (2003); *Re SK* (2005); *Re SA* (2005); *Re P (Forced Marriage)* (2010).) The Forced Marriage (Civil Protection) Act 2007 creates a new section 63A of the Family Law Act 1996, which enables the court to make a forced marriage protection order preventing an illegal forced marriage. An application can be brought by the victim or a relevant third party (e.g. a local authority).

Mental capacity to marry

The law here has a delicate balance to strike. On the one hand, if the requirement of mental capacity is too high, it will mean that people with mild learning difficulties will not be able to marry. On the other hand, set it too low and people with mental problems may be taken advantage of. The following case raised the issue well.

KEY CASE

Sheffield City Council v *E* [2005] Fam 326 (FD)

Concerning: capacity to marry

Facts

A local authority became concerned about a young woman who was 21 years old, but who had a variety of problems and functioned as a 13-year-old. She had befriended an older man who had a history of committing sexually violent crimes. They planned to marry. The local authority sought guidance on the degree of capacity required of her to be able to marry. ▶

> **Legal principle**
>
> Munby J stressed that it was presumed that a person had the capacity to marry. To have the capacity to marry, an individual had to understand the nature of marriage and the duties and responsibilities that flowed from it. These included that the man and woman agreed to live together; to love one another to the exclusion of all others in a relationship of mutual and reciprocal obligation; to share a common home and domestic life; and to enjoy each other's society, comfort and assistance. Munby J suggested that this was not meant to set the hurdle of capacity at a high level, and to understand these things did not require a high degree of intelligence. He also emphasised that the question of capacity to marry was different from the question of whether the person was wise to marry this person. Nor did capacity to marry require that the individual be aware of the characteristics of their proposed spouse.

Bars to annulment

Section 13 of the Matrimonial Causes Act 1973 sets down the bars to annulling a marriage. If one of these bars operates then, even though the applicant may be able to establish one of the voidable grounds, the court will not annul the marriage. The bars are:

■ Approbation. The petitioner knew that she could have avoided the marriage, but behaved in such a way that the respondent believed that she would not seek to annul the marriage. It must also be shown that it would be unjust to the respondent to grant the decree of annulment.

■ Three-year bar. If the applicant is relying on grounds (c), (d), (e), (f) or (h), then proceedings for annulment must be instituted within three years of the marriage.

■ Six-month bar. If (g) is relied upon (issue of an Interim Gender Recognition Certificate), then unless proceedings were instituted within six months of issuing the certificate, the court cannot annul the marriage.

■ Ignorance. In the case of (e), (f) and (h), the court cannot issue a decree unless satisfied that the petitioner was ignorant of the facts at the time of the marriage.

■ Civil partnership

Civil partnerships were created by the Civil Partnership Act 2004. They are only available to people of the same sex. We will have to see whether in future same-sex couples will prefer to marry rather than enter civil partnerships and so the institution falls out of favour.

KEY STATUTE

Civil Partnership Act 2004, section 3

'Two people are not eligible to register as civil partners of each other if –

(a) they are not of the same sex;

(b) either of them is already a civil partner or lawfully married;

(c) either of them is under 16; or

(d) they are within prohibited degrees of relationship.'

Differences between marriage and civil partnership	Sections of the statute (MCA: Matrimonial Causes Act 1973; CPA: Civil Partnership Act 2004)
Adultery is a fact that can be used to establish the ground for divorce	MCA, section 1(2)(a)
Adultery is not a fact that can be used to establish the ground for dissolution	CPA, section 44(5) lists the facts and adultery is not included
Non-consummation can be a ground for rendering a marriage voidable	MCA, section 12(a) and (b)
Non-consummation cannot be a ground for rendering a civil partnership voidable	CPA, section 50(1) lists the grounds and non-consummation is not included
The fact that the respondent has a venereal disease can render a marriage voidable	MCA, section 12(e)
The fact that the respondent has a venereal disease cannot render a civil partnership voidable	CPA, section 50(1) lists the grounds and venereal disease is not included

Civil partnerships are marriage in all but name. The table above sets out the few differences that exist between marriage and civil partnership. The Equality Act 2010 allows religious groups to include a civil partnership as part of a religious ceremony. That removed a distinction between marriage and civil partnership that used to exist, as previously a civil partnership could not be part of a religious service. You should learn these because an essay question on the topic may well require you to consider them.

■ The consequences of marriage and civil partnership

A popular question in an exam asks you to consider the differences between married and unmarried couples; or to consider the legal significance of marriage. Some of the most important consequences of marriage appear in the table below. The easiest way of explaining the significance of marriage and civil partnership is to contrast the law for spouses and civil partners with those who live together unmarried.

Marriage or civil partnership (CP)	Cohabitants
To enter or end a marriage or CP, formality requirements must be met	There are no formal requirements to start or end cohabitation!
At the end of a marriage or CP, the court has extensive powers to redistribute the couple's property and make maintenance orders	The court has no power to order maintenance to cohabitants nor redistribute property (although orders can be made in respect of children)
During marriage one spouse can seek financial support from the other (see e.g. Domestic Proceedings and Magistrates Courts Act 1978)	There is no obligation for a cohabitant to support the other financially
A father who is married to the mother of his child will automatically obtain parental responsibility	A man who is not married to the mother of his child will not automatically gain parental responsibility, but may acquire it by other means
When someone dies without a will, his or her spouse will automatically inherit all or most of the deceased's estate	When someone dies without a will, his or her cohabitant will not inherit anything automatically
There are tax benefits for spouses, particularly in relation to Capital Gains Tax or Inheritance Tax	There are no tax advantages for unmarried couples

✓ **Make your answer stand out**

1 Marriage means different things to different people. For some it is a religious sacrament, for others it is entered into purely for legal convenience. Is it possible to impose legal consequences for marriages, given its wide variety of meanings? When thinking about this you might want to consider some of the studies looking at why people marry (see Barlow *et al.* (2005)). These suggest widespread ignorance of the legal consequences of marriage.

2 If we were to do away with marriage as having any legal significance, what should replace it? There are plenty of suggestions: we could have civil partnership registration (this would enable the law to create a new marriage-like status that is free from the religious and social associations with marriage); we could use tort and contract law to deal with all disputes between couples (i.e. the law regulating couples would be the same as the law regulating two strangers); instead of focusing on sexual relationships between adults, we could focus on relationships of dependency, and so those relationships that were of significance to society would not be based on the husband–wife relationship but on the parent–child or carer– dependent-person relationship. This last idea is developed by Fineman (2004). Consider also the position of the two sisters in *Burden* v *UK* [2008] who had lived together for 31 years. They complained unsuccessfully to the European Court of Human Rights (ECHR) that they were unable to marry or enter a civil partnership. Should there be a way of legally recognising their relationship?

■ Putting it all together

Answer guidelines

See the essay question at the start of the chapter.

Approaching the question

A good answer will summarise the differences between marriage and civil partnership (see the table above). However, the essay asks you to discuss the differences, so more is needed than a summary of what they are. Here you can consider the two main views:

1 The differences are of no practical significance. For example, where there is adultery, the unreasonable behaviour fact can be relied upon.

▶

2 The differences are symbolically important because they relate to sex. They indicate that the law cannot accommodate, or feels uncomfortable about, same-sex relations.

Important points to include

The question also asks you about whether two people of the same sex should be allowed to marry. You should start by making it clear that following the Marriage (Same-Sex Couples) Act 2013 two people of the same sex can marry. The issues you will want to raise include the following:

- The religious significance of marriage and the fact that many religions would not accept same-sex marriage. Should religious objections be relevant to the law on marriage? Or does respect for religious belief require that grave offence is not caused?
- Discuss whether there should be a human right to marry who you wish to. What limits should be placed on that?
- Why is sex so important to marriage? Should it not be about tenderness, loving and caring, rather than whether or not there is a sexual component?

✓ Make your answer stand out

- Refer to studies on why people marry.
- Consider whether it is discrimination on the grounds of sex or sexual orientation for a same-sex couple not to marry.
- Ask yourself what would be lost if marriage ceased to have legal significance.

READ TO IMPRESS

Auchmuty, R. (2008) What's So Special About Marriage? The impact of *Wilkinson v Kitzinger*, *Child & Family Law Quarterly* (2008) 479–98.

Bamforth, N. (2007) 'The Benefits of Marriage in All but Name'? Same-sex Couples and the Civil Partnership Act 2004, *Child and Family Law Quarterly* 133.

Bamforth, N. (2011) Families, But Not Yet Marriages, *Child and Family Law Quarterly* 73.

Barker, N. J. (2012) *Not The Marrying Kind: A Feminist Critique of Same-Sex Marriage*, Basingstoke: Palgrave.

Barlow, A., Duncan, S., James, G. and Park, A. (2005) *Cohabitation, Marriage and the Law*. Oxford: Hart.

Bernstein, A. (ed.) (2006) *Marriage Proposals: Questioning A Legal Status*. New York: New York University Press.

Chau, P.-L. and Herring, J. (2002) Defining, Assigning and Designing Sex,16 *International Journal of Law, Policy and the Family* 327.

Cretney, S. (2006) *Same-Sex Relationships*. Oxford: OUP.

Fineman, M. (2004) *The Autonomy Myth*. New York: OUP.

Glennon, L. (2010) The Limitations of Equality Discourses on the Contours of Intimate Obligations, in Wallbank, J., Choudhry, S. and Herring, J. (eds) *Rights, Gender and Family Law*. Abingdon: Routledge.

Herring, J., Barker, H. and Fox, M. (2010) Sheffield CC v E in Hunter, R., McGlynn, C. and Rackley, E. (eds) Feminist Judgments, Oxford: Hart.

www.pearsoned.co.uk/lawexpress

Go online to access more revision support including quizzes to test your knowledge, sample questions with answer guidelines, podcasts you can download, and more!

Cohabitation

2

Revision checklist

Essential points you should know:

- [ ] The difference in legal treatment of cohabitees and married couples or civil partners
- [ ] When the law treats unmarried couples and married couples in the same way
- [ ] The law on resulting trusts, constructive trusts and proprietary estoppel
- [ ] Proposed reforms of the law on cohabitation

■ Topic map

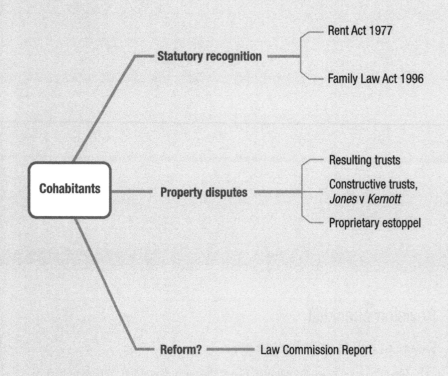

Statutory recognition
— Rent Act 1977
— Family Law Act 1996

Cohabitants

Property disputes
— Resulting trusts
— Constructive trusts, *Jones* v *Kernott*
— Proprietary estoppel

Reform? ——— Law Commission Report

A printable version of this topic map is available from **www.pearsoned.co.uk/lawexpress**

■ Introduction

Many cohabiting couples believe that they have the same rights as married couples, but they are badly mistaken.

An increasing number of couples are living together without getting married or entering a civil partnership. The days when 'living in sin' (outside marriage) was widely seen as wicked are gone, but that does not mean the law equates cohabitation with marriage or civil partnership. In some areas married and unmarried couples are treated in the same way but in others they are not. There is widespread agreement that the current regulation of couples who are not married or civil partners is unsatisfactory. However, there is hot debate over how the law should be reformed. At the heart of this debate is the problem that within the category of 'unmarried couples' there is a whole range of different kinds of relationships.

ASSESSMENT ADVICE

Essay questions

A popular essay question asks students to summarise the differences between the way the law treats married and unmarried couples and to discuss whether there should be any differences. A good answer will consider the Law Commission Consultation Report (2007) on the topic. You should avoid assuming the answer is a straightforward: 'unmarried couples should be treated in the same way as married couples' or 'unmarried couples should not be treated in the same way as married couples'. It may be that there are some areas of the law where the two should be treated in the same way and others where they should not. Some commentators, for example, suggest that in relation to child matters no difference should be drawn, but in relation to financial matters there should be a difference.

Problem questions

A popular area for problem questions is property rights of unmarried couples. This requires an excellent knowledge of the law on resulting trusts, constructive trusts and proprietary estoppel. A good answer will seek to demonstrate that the courts are not always consistent in this area and will use the case law to make the arguments both for and against there being a property interest.

■ Sample question

Could you answer this question? Below is a typical problem question that could arise on this topic. Guidelines on answering the question are included at the end of this chapter; a sample essay question and guidance on tackling it can be found on the companion website.

PROBLEM QUESTION

Alan owns a large detached house, which is registered in his name alone. He meets Steve at a night club and invites him to stay in his house. Over breakfast the next morning Alan says to Steve: 'I love you and everything I have is yours.' Steve moves in and they live as a couple. Alan tells Steve that if he does domestic chores about the house, he will make sure that he does not go unrewarded. Steve undertakes the housework and pays for several bills. Once he gives Alan some cash as a gift because Alan says he is so hard up that he is struggling to meet the mortgage payments. Steve does some decoration and puts up a shed in the garden. Three years later over supper Alan proposes to Steve and says 'I want you to share ownership of the house.' Steve says, 'But I thought the house was ours already.' This leads to a huge row and Alan throws Steve out of the house, saying their relationship is over. Does Steve have any property interest in the house?

■ Cohabitation and the law: the general approach

Cohabitants can find themselves at a disadvantage when compared to spouses (as we saw in Chapter 1). They cannot claim maintenance or property adjustment orders on divorce. And they are not entitled to anything automatically if their partner dies without making a will. Indeed, they are treated in the same way as strangers in the law unless there is a statutory provision saying otherwise.

In this chapter we will particularly focus on what happens to property when an unmarried couple split up. This is the most common kind of dispute to reach the courts and the most likely issue to arise in a problem question in an exam. But first we will also look at the statutory recognition of cohabitants.

▓ Statutory recognition of cohabitation

In a number of statutes, Parliament has given the same rights to spouses as to people who are living together as if they are married. For example, under the Family Law Act 1996 (see Chapter 3) cohabitants have the same rights as spouses or civil partners to apply for a non-molestation order. The following case represents a significant extension of statutory recognition of cohabitation.

KEY CASE

Ghaidan v *Godin-Mendoza* [2004] 2 AC 557 (HL)
Concerning: definition of 'living together as husband and wife'

Facts

Mr Wallwyn-James was the tenant of a flat. For nearly 20 years he lived there with Mr Godin-Mendoza before he died. Mr Godin-Mendoza claimed that he was entitled to take over the tenancy under the terms of the Rent Act 1977 because he was living 'as husband and wife' with the tenant.

Legal principle

Relying on the Human Rights Act 1998, the House of Lords was willing to interpret the phrase 'living together as husband and wife' to include a same-sex couple. The interpretation was required to avoid discrimination against people on the basis of their sexual orientation. Further, the public policy behind allowing unmarried opposite-sex cohabitants to succeed to tenancies applied equally to same-sex cohabitants.

✔ Make your answer stand out

A common essay question asks you to consider whether the law on cohabitation needs reform. Do you think there is a case for saying that unmarried couples should be treated just like married couples for all matters in relation to children, but differently in relation to financial matters between themselves? Is it possible to make this distinction: does not a parent's financial position affect a child? Should children have a right to be treated in the same way, regardless of the marital status of their parents? How would the law be different if we took this principle seriously? Would the proposals in the Law Commission Report improve the law if they were implemented?

■ Property disputes between cohabiting couples

When cohabiting couples separate, all the courts can do is to declare who owns what. There is no power to change ownership in the way the courts can do with civil partners or spouses. Nearly all of the cases that have reached the law reports are cases involving disputes over the ownership of the home. So we shall focus on those.

In relation to land (which includes buildings on land) the starting point is who owns the property at common law. This is ascertained by reference in most cases to the Land Registry: the person who is registered as the owner is the legal owner. If the land is unregistered, then it is the person into whose name the property was last **conveyed**. However, the ownership of legal title is only the start of the process, because the owner may be holding the property on trust. In other words, the sole legal owner may not own all the equitable interest in the property. In the case of land, express trusts can only be created in writing. If there is no express trust, then it is necessary to consider whether there is an implied trust: a **resulting trust**; a **constructive trust**; or a **proprietary estoppel**.

✎ EXAM TIP

In an exam, remember to consider each of the three ways an interest may be claimed: a resulting trust, a constructive trust and a proprietary estoppel. However, it is worth noting that the courts have accepted that there is a great deal of overlap between these concepts. So do not be surprised if in a case you find there is, say, both a constructive trust and a proprietary estoppel, or indeed all three!

📖 REVISION NOTE

Don't forget that if there are children, child support may have to be paid under the Child Support Act 1991, even where the couple are unmarried. Also that under section 15 of and Schedule 1 to the Children Act 1989, the court can order lump sums or property transfers for the benefit of the child. That power, however, cannot be used to provide accommodation just for a partner; it needs to be shown that the property is required for the child. These statutes are discussed in Chapter 5.

Resulting trusts

KEY DEFINITION: Resulting trust

A resulting trust is presumed to arise when A contributes to the purchase price of a piece of property that is put into B's name; or A transfers property to B, receiving nothing in return. In these cases it is presumed that B holds on trust for A. This presumption can be rebutted if there is evidence that the parties did not intend to create a trust.

The presumption of a resulting trust applies where a person gives another property for nothing in return or where a person contributes to the purchase of property that is put in another's name. Notice, however, that the courts have said that the presumption should only be used as a last resort and where there is no evidence to suggest what the real intentions of the parties were. In *Jones* v *Kernott* the Supreme Court held that it would rarely be helpful to use resulting trust in a case involving a cohabiting couple.

Constructive trusts

KEY DEFINITION: Constructive trust

In order to establish a constructive trust, it is necessary to show:

1. A common intention to share ownership. This is proved by evidence of an express agreement to share ownership or it can be inferred from a direct contribution to the purchase price or mortgage instalment.
2. Actions by the claimant in reliance on the common intention.

KEY CASE

Lloyds Bank Plc v *Rosset* [1991] 1 AC 107 (HL)

Concerning: constructive trusts

Facts

In a dispute between Mr and Mrs Rosset and their bank, which had a mortgage over their house, a key issue arose: did Mrs Rosset have an interest under a constructive trust? The legal title of the house was in Mr Rosset's name alone. Mrs Rosset had supervised builders carrying out work on the property and done some decoration on it. She had never discussed ownership of the property with her husband.

Legal principle

In order to establish a constructive trust, it must be shown that there was an express agreement to share ownership of the property. In the absence of an actual conversation, such an agreement could only be inferred from a contribution to the purchase price or mortgage instalment. Mrs Rosset, therefore, was not entitled to claim an interest under a constructive trust.

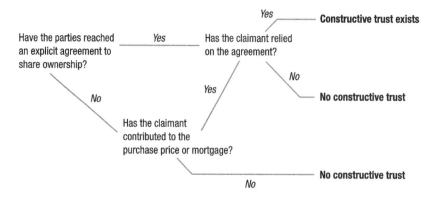

The first element of a constructive trust is that there is a common intention to share ownership. The courts have, in fact, been generous in finding from casual snippets of conversation that the couple expressly agreed to share ownership, and the following have been accepted as sufficient:

- Where the man (untruthfully) said to the woman that she was too young to be allowed to be put on the title deeds, the court held that the fact that he used this excuse indicated that there was an agreement to share (*Eves* v *Eves* (1975)).

- Where, although the woman had not paid towards the purchase price of the property or the mortgage, she had talked with her partner about ownership and they had agreed to share (*Cox* v *Jones* (2004)).

The traditional approach to constructive trusts suggests that in cases where there has been no financial contribution and there is no evidence of an explicit agreement to share, there can be no constructive trust (*Churchill* v *Roach* (2004)). However, some recent cases have suggested the courts might be willing to find evidence of an agreement to share from the way the couple arranged their finances (*Abbott* v *Abbott* (2007)). Note also that what must be found is an agreement to share ownership, not just an agreement to share occupation.

> ✓ **Make your answer stand out**
>
> **Indirect contributions**
> There has been much dispute over whether it is possible to infer an agreement to share ownership from an indirect contribution to a mortgage instalment. For example, where the claimant has paid other household bills and the owner has only been able to meet the mortgage payments because the claimant has paid these. In *Rosset*, Lord Bridge required a 'direct' contribution to a mortgage payment. However, there is one first-instance decision which held that an indirect contribution would suffice (*Le Foe* v *Le Foe* (2002)). Watch out for this issue arising in a problem question in the exam.

If it is possible to find evidence of the common intention to share ownership and there has been reliance on it, the court must then ascertain what share each party has under a constructive trust. Where the parties have agreed what shares they have, the law will reflect the agreement. Where they have not agreed, then the court must decide what the parties' intentions were (*Stack* v *Dowden* (2007)). Where the property has been bought in joint names it will be presumed that the parties intended to share the property, unless there is evidence to suggest otherwise (*Stack* v *Dowden* (2007)).

KEY CASE

Jones v *Kernott* [2011] UKSC 53

Concerning: When to find a constructive trust

Facts

In 1985 Mr Kernott and Ms Jones bought a house together in joint names. Ms Jones paid the outgoings on the property, including the mortgage. Mr Kernott gave money to Ms Jones to cover general expenses and did a substantial amount of building work. They had two children before the relationship ended in 1993. Mr Kernott then moved out and Ms Jones continued to pay the mortgage and other expenses connected with the property but Mr Kernott no longer paid towards the house. In 2008 proceedings were commenced disputing the ownership of the house. Ms Jones claimed that she owned 90% of the beneficial interest, while Mr Kernott claimed 50%.

Legal principle

In cases where a couple purchased a property in joint names there was a presumption that the couple intended to share the beneficial ownership equally. That presumption could be rebutted if there is evidence that the couple intended to share in different proportions. That intention may arise some time after the purchase. The court would consider whether there was evidence of their actual intentions (e.g. through conversations). If that could not be found the court would infer their intentions from their conduct and the nature of their relationship. In the absence of evidence as to their actual intentions the court could impute the intention that the couple would share the property in a fair way. Applying this approach to this case, the couple would be taken to have shared the property 90% to Ms Jones and 10% to Mr Kernott. Lord Wilson appeared to do this on the basis of an imputed intention. Lady Hale and Lord Walker appeared to rely on an inferred intention.

! Don't be tempted to . . .

Determining shares under a constructive trust

The House of Lords in *Jones* v *Kernott* (2011) accepted that if there is no evidence as to the parties' intentions it should be assumed that they would want to share the property in a fair way. Notice, however, that this imputed intention should be used only as a last resort. This seems reasonable. It is not unreasonable to assume that the parties in a close relationship would want to treat each other fairly.

Proprietary estoppel

KEY DEFINITION: Proprietary estoppel

For X to be able to establish a proprietary estoppel it must be shown that:

1 the owner of the property assured or promised X an interest in the property;
2 X reasonably relied on the promise to her detriment;
3 it would be unconscionable not to give X an interest in the property.

The courts have said that the notion of **conscionability** (fairness) is at the heart of estoppel (*Gillett* v *Holt* (2000)). In other words, there may be a degree of flexibility about the requirements if justice demands that the claimant be given an interest in the property. So in an exam it may be worth making the point that even if the promise is a little unclear, an argument could be made that the court will still find an estoppel if, given the amount of detrimental reliance, it would be unfair not to (*Wayling* v *Jones* (1995)). The following case is a classic example of how a proprietary estoppel can arise.

KEY CASE

Thorner v *Major* **[2009] UKHL 18 (HL)**

Concerning: proprietary estoppel

Facts

Mr Thorner had worked on his cousin's farm for 29 years without pay. The cousin was said to be a man of few words. He led Thorner to believe that he would leave him the farm under his will, after giving a life insurance policy to Thorner 'to pay for death duties'. In fact, when the cousin died, it was found he had made a will leaving the farm to his siblings.

Legal principle

For a statement to form the basis of a proprietary estoppel claim it had to be 'clear enough'. Whether it was clear would depend on the context of the words or actions. That meant that it would be wrong to say the statement had to be 'clear and unambiguous'. Normally it would be enough if the claimant could show it was reasonable for the claimant to take the works or conduct as an assurance upon which she could rely. In this case the fact the cousin was not talkative was a relevant factor. Ultimately the claim failed on the basis that the cousin had never made it clear what property would be left to Thorner. A promise that a person would inherit something, without making it clear what land was being referred to, could not form the basis of a proprietary estoppel claim.

Reform of the law

Contrast the position of an unmarried couple who have separated with that of a married couple. For a married couple or civil partners, the court can divide up the property in order to achieve the result that is fair. For a cohabiting couple, the court is restricted to deciding who owns what under the law of trusts. However, some commentators suggest that the law of trusts in this area has developed in a sufficiently flexible way to enable the courts to reach the same decision for unmarried couples as for married couples.

The Law Commission has produced a report (2007) on the issue. It suggests that the court should have the power to redistribute the ownership of the home when a cohabiting couple separates. This can be done in order to ensure that one party does not suffer due to an economic sacrifice he or she has made during the relationship (e.g. in giving up a career in order to look after children) or that one party does not unjustifiably retain an economic benefit made during the relationship.

✓ **Make your answer stand out**

Read the Law Commission report in this area. How would you respond to the proposals? Do you think the proposals will change the results that the courts are reaching or will the main impact be in making the courts more open about what they are doing? Is it right that couples should be able to opt out of the proposed scheme? Why do you think the proposal that cohabiting couples be treated in exactly the same way as married couples in this area has received so little support?

Cohabitation contracts

A married couple cannot sign a binding pre-marriage or pre-nuptial contract that will prevent the courts from deciding how to distribute their property on divorce. However, an unmarried couple are allowed to sign a cohabitation contract which sets out what will happen to their property when they separate. If the contract is valid under the normal rules of contract law (e.g. there was no misrepresentation), then the contract can be enforced. The following is a startling case on cohabitation contracts.

KEY CASE

Sutton v *Mishcon de Reya* [2004] 1 FLR 837 (FD)

Concerning: enforceability of cohabitation contracts

Facts

Mr Sutton and Mr Stahl wished to sign a cohabitation contract. They approached the defendant firm of solicitors and asked them to draw up a contract that would acknowledge they were in a master–slave relationship. They wanted the contract to say, for example, that Stahl would obey all of Sutton's commands. The solicitors warned that the contract was probably unenforceable. When the couple separated this turned out to be true and Sutton sued the solicitors in negligence.

Legal principle

Normally, cohabitation contracts were enforceable. However, contracts for sexual services were not. In this case the sexual side of the relationship was apparent throughout the contract. It would not have been possible, therefore, to produce an enforceable contract of the kind Sutton asked for.

■ Putting it all together

Answer guidelines

See the problem question at the start of the chapter.

Approaching the question

In this problem question you will need to start by ascertaining who has the legal title to the property – that is, who the registered owner is. In this case, it is Alan. There is no express trust and so the only claims that Steve may make are for implied trusts.

Important points to include

Resulting trust: Steve cannot claim a resulting trust as there is no contribution to the purchase price.

Constructive trust: Steve will need to show there is a common intention. He could raise three arguments. First, that the common intention to share is revealed by the statement: 'I love you and everything I have is yours.' Or second, he could argue that there should be an inferred agreement based on the payment of the household bills (contrast *Rosset* and *Le Foe*). Or third, he could rely on the statement: 'I want you to share ownership of the house.' He would also need to show reliance. Paying the bills and doing housework may well be sufficient. But, notice that in relation to the third statement, there does not appear to be any reliance on the agreement after it was reached. So that may well mean that the third argument will not succeed.

Proprietary estoppel: Steve will need to show a promise or assurance. He could rely on Alan's breakfast statement or on the statement about 'not going unrewarded'. As to the latter notice, the statement does not relate clearly to the property and this will greatly weaken his case (see *Lissimore* v *Downing* (2003); *Thorner* v *Major* (2009)). He could rely on the supper statement, but there is no obvious detrimental reliance.

✓ Make your answer stand out

■ Make sure you include a wide range of case law.

■ Discuss the uncertainties in the case law over when an agreement can be inferred or found.

■ Remember to explain the arguments that could be made on both sides.

READ TO IMPRESS

Bailey-Harris, R. (1996) Law and the Unmarried Couple – Oppression or Liberation?, *Child and Family Law Quarterly* 137.

Bridge, S. (2007) Cohabitation: Why Legislative Reform is Necessary, *Family Law* 911.

Duncan, S., Barlow, A. and James, G. (2005) Why Don't They Marry? Cohabitation, Commitment and DIY Marriage, *Child and Family Law Quarterly* 383.

Gardner, S. (2008) Family Property Today, *Law Quarterly Review* 263.

Herring, J. (2013) *Caring and the Law,* Oxford: Hart.

Law Commission (2007) *Cohabitation: The Financial Consequences of Relationship Breakdown.*

Lewis, J. (1999) Marriage and Cohabitation and the Nature of Commitment, *Child and Family Law Quarterly* 355.

Mee, J. (2009) The Limits of Propriety Estoppel, *Child and Family Law Quarterly* 367.

Miles, J. (2005) Property Law v Family Law: Resolving the Problems of Family Property, *Legal Studies* 624.

www.pearsoned.co.uk/lawexpress

Go online to access more revision support including quizzes to test your knowledge, sample questions with answer guidelines, podcasts you can download, and more!

Domestic violence

3

Revision checklist

Essential points you should know:

☐ The range of orders available under the Family Law Act 1996

☐ The grounds for the orders available under the Family Law Act 1996

☐ The role of the criminal law in domestic violence

☐ The policy tensions in domestic violence law

▉ Topic map

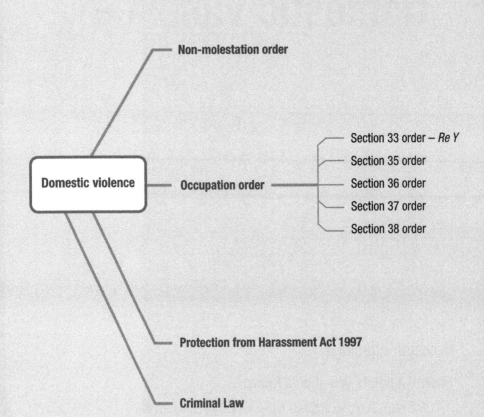

- Non-molestation order
- Occupation order
  - Section 33 order – *Re Y*
  - Section 35 order
  - Section 36 order
  - Section 37 order
  - Section 38 order
- Protection from Harassment Act 1997
- Criminal Law

Domestic violence

A printable version of this topic map is available from **www.pearsoned.co.uk/lawexpress**

■ Introduction

You are quite likely to be the victim of domestic violence at some point in your life: one in four women and one in six men are.

Domestic violence is a major social problem that raises a host of complex legal issues. An incident of domestic violence can lead to consequences in criminal law and civil law. Both will need to be considered when answering exam questions. The remedies in civil law are found in the Family Law Act 1996 and the Protection from Harassment Act 1997. For an exam you will need to be aware not only of the statutory and case law material, but also the theoretical issues surrounding the topic.

ASSESSMENT ADVICE

Essay questions

As well as being aware of the actual law, essays on domestic violence might also ask you to consider why the law has been slow to respond to domestic violence and what problems the law has faced in responding to it – in particular, the troublesome cases where the victim does not want legal intervention. Should the law respect her wishes or protect her from violence even if she does not want to be protected? You should be aware of the academic discussions on this issue.

A really good answer to an essay would include some of the material on the causes of domestic violence: is it a reflection of society's attitudes to women in general (see Freeman, 1984) or is it a personality disorder that is best dealt with by counselling? Also there is much debate on what constitutes domestic violence: where is the line to be drawn between domestic violence and a crime between strangers (see Reece (2006) and Madden Dempsey (2006))? You would impress an examiner if you were aware of some of these writings.

Problem questions

Problem questions on domestic violence require a good knowledge of the provisions of the Family Law Act 1996 and the Protection from Harassment Act 1997. You need to start by considering for which orders the applicant can apply and under which sections. You will then need to state the factors the court must consider when deciding whether or not to make an order, using case law where useful. Don't forget to explain the effect of the order once it has been made.

Sample question

Could you answer this problem question? Below is a typical problem question that could arise on this topic. Guidelines on answering the question are included at the end of this chapter; a sample essay question and guidance on tackling it can be found on the companion website.

PROBLEM QUESTION

Amy and Brent are in a committed relationship. They have been living together for four years. Their house is in Brent's name, but they regard it as jointly owned. Over the past few months Brent has become increasingly aggressive towards Amy. He has shouted at her and thrown things across the room. Amy has recently discovered that she is pregnant and is terrified that Brent might do something that will hurt the baby. When he learned of the pregnancy, Brent started to attend anger-management classes and these have helped him to control his anger. After a particularly stressful day at work, Brent threw a glass onto the ground and it broke, cutting Amy. Amy ran out of the house and is currently staying at a friend's house on her sofa. Amy seeks advice on what orders she could apply for in order to protect herself. Ideally, she would like to return to the house.

Defining domestic violence

At one time domestic violence was thought to be restricted to married couples.

KEY CASE

Yemshaw v *London Borough of Hounslow* [2011] UKSC 3

Concerning: the definition of domestic violence

Facts

Mrs Yemshaw sought housing from her local authority. As she could live in the marital home, she could only claim to be homeless if she was the victim of domestic violence. She accepted that her husband had not been physically violent to her but claimed she was terrified of him and that he had been emotionally abusive towards her. The Council took the view that domestic violence was restricted to cases of physical abuse. Mrs Yemshaw challenged that approach in the court.

> **Legal principle**
>
> Domestic violence should be given a broad interpretation and is not restricted to cases of physical violence. It could include making someone fearful of violence or giving rise to a risk of violence. It could include denigration of the victim's personality, or depriving them of their liberty.

Civil orders under the Family Law Act 1996

Remember that there are two kinds of order under the Family Law Act 1996: the non-molestation order and the occupation order.

The non-molestation order

KEY DEFINITION: Molestation

> Molestation includes acts that harass or threaten the victim. It must be conduct that is not simply an invasion of privacy.

An applicant can only seek a non-molestation order against a person with whom he or she is associated. There are eight categories of associated people (defined in section 62 of the Family Law Act):

1 They are or have been married to each other or entered a civil partnership together.

2 They are cohabitants or former cohabitants.

3 They live in the same household, other than merely by reason of one of them being the other's employee, tenant, lodger or boarder.

4 They are relatives. This is broadly defined and even includes nieces and nephews.

5 They have agreed to marry one another or enter a civil partnership together. Section 44 of the Family Law Act 1996 contains strict rules about proving such agreements.

6 They have or have had an intimate personal relationship with each other that is or was of significant duration.

7 Where the applicant is a child, a person who has parental responsibility for the child.

8 They are parties to the same family proceedings.

✎ EXAM TIP

> Remember to consider carefully whether the applicant and respondent are associated people. If they are not, you should consider whether the applicant can bring an application for an order under the Protection from Harassment Act 1997, where there is no need for proof that the parties were associated.

If the applicant and respondent are associated, the court can consider whether or not to make a non-molestation order, based on section 42(5), Family Law Act 1996. To be honest, this is not a particularly helpful provision, stating that the court must consider all the circumstances of the case. But it does emphasise the importance that harm to children can play when the court is considering an application. Section 42A, Family Law Act 1996 makes it a criminal offence to breach a non-molestation order.

KEY STATUTE

Family Law Act 1996, section 42(5)

In deciding whether or not to make a non-molestation order, the court 'shall have regard to all the circumstances including the need to secure the health, safety and well-being —

(a) of the applicant [. . .] and

(b) of any relevant child'.

KEY CASE

C v C (Non-Molestation Order: Jurisdiction) [1998] 1 FCR 11 (HC)

Concerning: the meaning of molestation

Facts

The wife had communicated with journalists about her relationship with her husband. He sought a non-molestation order to prevent her from making revelations in newspapers about their life together.

Legal principle

The husband failed in his application. Merely disclosing a person's private affairs was not molestation. Molestation required 'some quite deliberate conduct which is aimed at a high degree of harassment of the other party'.

Occupation orders

Occupation orders can be sought under sections 33, 35, 36, 37 and 38.

✎ EXAM TIP

This is a confusing area of the law, but if you have a clear idea of who can use which section, you will impress the examiners. Note that in order to decide whether an applicant is entitled, you may need to refer to the law on ownership of the home, discussed in Chapter 2.

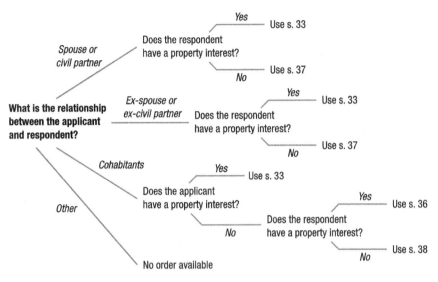

Section 33 applications

To be able to use section 33, the applicant must be an entitled applicant. This concept is defined in section 33.

KEY STATUTE

Family Law Act 1996, section 33(1)

'An entitled person is one who:

(i) is entitled to occupy a dwelling-house by virtue of a beneficial estate or interest or contract or by virtue of any enactment giving him the right to remain in occupation; or

(ii) has home rights in relation to a dwelling-house.'

Notice that virtually all spouses and civil partners will have an interest in their home or a home right and, therefore, will be entitled. Cohabitants will need to show that they have an interest in the property, for example, by way of a constructive trust.

☐ REVISION NOTE

To see whether or not a cohabitant has an interest in the property and so can rely on section 33, you may need to refer to the law on constructive and resulting trusts. See Chapter 2.

In considering an applicant under section 33, the court will start by considering whether the 'significant harm test' in section 33(8) is satisfied. This requires the court to consider two questions:

- Question 1: 'Will the applicant or relevant child suffer significant harm attributable to the conduct of the respondent if an order is not made?'
- Question 2: 'Will the respondent or relevant child suffer significant harm if the order is made?'

If the answer to Question 1 is 'no', then the significant harm test is not satisfied and the court is not compelled to make an order. However, if the answer is 'yes', then the court must compare the harm the applicant and child will suffer if the order is not made and the harm the respondent and child will suffer if the order is made. If the harm to the applicant and child will be greater, the court must make an order. If not, then the court does not have to make an order.

If the significant harm test is not satisfied, the court must consider whether or not to make an order considering the general factors in section 33(6). These are:

- the housing needs and housing resources of each of the parties and of any relevant child;
- the financial resources of each of the parties;
- the likely effect of any order, or of any decision by the court not to exercise its powers on the health, safety or well-being of the parties and of any relevant child; and
- the conduct of the parties in relation to each other and otherwise.

▮ Don't be tempted to . . .

Interpreting the significant harm test
Four errors are commonly made by students when considering the grounds for making a section 33 order.

First, students sometimes make the mistake of thinking that if the significant harm test is not satisfied, then an occupation order cannot be made. The Court of Appeal in *Chalmers* v *Johns* (1999) emphasised that even if the significant harm test is not satisfied, the court could still make an occupation order if that was appropriate after considering the general factors in section 33(6).

Second, note that in the significant harm test the applicant's significant harm must be attributable to the conduct of the respondent. Do not assume that the test is satisfied just because the applicant is suffering significant harm. The respondent must have been at least partly to blame for the harm.

Third, notice that in deciding whether to make an order the court should consider the needs of the applicant and not what might be pleasant for the applicant (*G* v *G* (2009)).

Fourth, remember that the needs of children must be taken into account, as well as the needs of adults (*Re L (Occupation Order)* (2012)).

Remember that there is a wide variety of forms of occupation order under section 33(3), ranging from removing the respondent from the house to excluding him or her from part of the house. They include:

- enforcing the applicant's right to remain in the property;

- requiring the respondent to allow the applicant to enter and remain in the house;

- regulating the occupation of the home (e.g. by allowing the respondent to live in one half of the house and the applicant in the other);

- requiring the respondent to leave the home and suspending or restricting his right to occupy;

- excluding the respondent from a defined area around the home.

KEY CASE

Re Y (Children) (Occupation Order) [2000] 2 FCR 470 (CA)
Concerning: when an occupation order should be made

Facts

The husband and wife's relationship had broken down and there was constant shouting and arguing in the house. The two children sided with different parents. The atmosphere in the house was, according to the trial judge, 'intolerable'.

Legal principle

The Court of Appeal held that an occupation order should not be made. Occupation orders were 'draconian' and were to be used as a last resort in exceptional cases. This case involved the ordinary tensions of divorce.

Section 35 applications

Section 35 is to be used by ex-spouses or ex-civil partners who have no right to occupy. The grounds for making an order are similar to those for section 33. But there are some extra general factors to consider, listed in section 35(6), such as the length of time since the marriage or civil partnership was dissolved.

Section 36 applications

Section 36 is available for **cohabitants** or former cohabitants who do not have a property interest. For these applicants the significant harm test does not apply, but rather the court must consider whether the applicant will suffer significant harm without an order and the impact of any order on the respondent.

KEY DEFINITION: Cohabitants

Cohabitants are 'two persons who, although not married to each other, are living together as husband and wife or (if of the same sex) in an equivalent relationship' (section 62(1)(a), Family Law Act 1996).

Section 37 and 38 applications

These are rarely used because they apply where neither the respondent nor applicant is entitled to live in the property in question. This would be relevant if they were squatting somewhere.

EXAM TIP

We have highlighted here in brief some of the major differences in the grounds for making the occupation orders under each section and the kinds of orders that can be made. An excellent candidate will be aware of all of the differences between the sections.

 Make your answer stand out

The Family Law Act draws a distinction between applicants based on whether or not they have property interests and whether or not they are (or have been) married. Do you think either of these is an appropriate ground for distinguishing between applicants? In the debates while the legislation was going through Parliament, the argument that treating married and unmarried couples in the same way in this area would undermine marriage proved influential. Do you think that was a good argument? Issues like this may well come up in the exam.

■ Civil orders under the Protection from Harassment Act 1997

Another source of protection under the civil law is the Protection from Harassment Act. The court can make an order restraining the respondent from harassing the victim and even require the payment of compensation. To obtain a restraining order it must be shown that the respondent has infringed section 1 of the Act or is about to.

KEY STATUTE

Protection from Harassment Act 1997, section 1(1)

'A person must not pursue a course of conduct –

(a) which amounts to harassment of another, and

(b) which he knows or ought to know amounts to harassment of another.'

✎ EXAM TIP

Remember that section 1 is only breached if there is a course of conduct. There are quite a number of cases defining what a 'course of conduct' is (including *Lau* v *DPP*, below). You should have as good a knowledge of this case law as possible.

KEY CASE

Lau v *DPP* **[2000] 1 FLR 799 (QBD)**

Concerning: the meaning of 'a course of conduct'

Facts

The defendant slapped his girlfriend. Four months later he was verbally abusive to her in the street. He was charged with the offence under section 1 of the Protection from Harassment Act 1997.

Legal principle

He was not guilty of the offence. There was an insufficient nexus between the two pieces of conduct to make them a 'course of conduct'. There was quite a gap in time between the incidents and they were not similar in nature.

■ Criminal proceedings following an incident of domestic violence

The fact that a violent incident has occurred in a home or between a couple does not affect its position in the criminal law. So all the offences that can be committed between strangers can be committed between couples. Under the Crime and Security Act 2010 a police officer can issue a domestic violence protection notice, if she believes that someone has been the victim of violence and the notice will protect them. If that is breached, then a court can make a domestic violence protection order, which can restrict behaviour that might endanger the victim.

✎ EXAM TIP

Although, in theory, a crime in the home is as much a crime as one in the street, there is much evidence that this is not true in practice. A good answer would refer to the academic material that discusses the ways in which the police, prosecutors and the courts have failed to take domestic violence seriously (see Hoyle and Sanders (2000)). However, some police forces do now seem to be trying to tackle the problem and have set up domestic violence units.

✓ **Make your answer stand out**

Consider what should happen if the police arrest a man who is being violent to his partner, but she does not want the police to prosecute. There is fierce academic debate as to how to proceed in a case like this. On the one hand, there are those who state that the 'victim' of domestic violence has the right to decide how she wants the situation dealt with. Her decision should be respected (see Hoyle and Sanders (2000)). On the other hand, there are those who urge that there should be a prosecution (if possible) even if the victim says that she does not want that. Choudhry and Herring (2006) argue that this is required in cases of serious violence under the Human Rights Act 1998 (*Opuz* v *Turkey* (2009)).

■ Putting it all together

Answer guidelines

See the problem question at the start of the chapter.

Approaching the question

It is important to consider all the orders that could be sought. For each, make sure you explain clearly the grounds that need to be established and the effect of the order.

Important points to include

Remember to discuss the three possible orders that can be sought:

■ Non-molestation order. The courts are normally willing to make these orders where there has been violence or threatening behaviour. After all, it is not a great infringement of the respondent's freedom if he cannot molest the respondent.

■ Protection from harassment. There appears to be a course of conduct (you could briefly discuss the case law on the definition of this).

■ Occupation order. You need to start by deciding which section Amy can use. To use section 33 she will need to establish an interest in the property. She could try to argue there is a constructive trust (see Chapter 2), but remember there must be an agreement, rather than an unspoken assumption about ownership. If there is no constructive trust, she needs to use section 36 (*Chalmers* v *Johns* (1999)). Remember that the significant harm test applies to section 33 (*G* v *G* (2009)), but you only have the significant harm questions under section 36.

✓ **Make your answer stand out**

There are some interesting issues to discuss with the significant harm test.

■ Can harm to the foetus be significant harm? Or could the application rely on harm in the future to the child when born?

■ Is Amy's harm significant? Is it attributable to Brent?

■ Is it relevant that Brent has taken steps to control his temper?

READ TO IMPRESS

Burton, M. (2008) *Legal Responses to Domestic Violence*. London: Routledge.

Choudhry, S. (2010) Mandatory Prosecution and Arrest, in Wallbank, J., Choudhry, S. and Herring, J. (eds) *Rights, Gender and Family Law*. Abingdon: Routledge.

Choudhry, S. and Herring, J. (2006) Righting Domestic Violence, 20 *International Journal of Law, Policy and the Family* 95.

Freeman, M. (1984) Legal Ideologies: Patriarchal Precedents and Domestic Violence, in Freeman, M. (ed.) *The State, the Law and the Family*. London: Sweet and Maxwell.

Herring, J. (2011) The Meaning of Domestic Violence, *Journal of Social Welfare and Family Law* 297.

Hoyle, C. and Sanders, A. (2000) Police Responses to Domestic Violence: from Victim Choice to Victim Empowerment, 40 *British Journal of Criminology* 14.

Madden Dempsey, M. (2006) What Counts as Domestic Violence? A Conceptual Analysis, 12 *William and Mary Journal of Women and the Law* 301.

Madden Dempsey, M. (2009) *Prosecuting Domestic Violence*. Oxford: OUP.

Reece, H. (2006) The End of Domestic Violence, 69 *Modern Law Review* 770.

www.pearsoned.co.uk/lawexpress

Go online to access more revision support including quizzes to test your knowledge, sample questions with answer guidelines, podcasts you can download, and more!

Divorce and
dissolution

4

Revision checklist

Essential points you should know:

- [ ] The ground for divorce
- [ ] The facts establishing the ground
- [ ] The meaning of adultery
- [ ] The meaning of the behaviour ground
- [ ] Proposals for reform of divorce law
- [ ] Dissolution for civil partnerships

■ Topic map

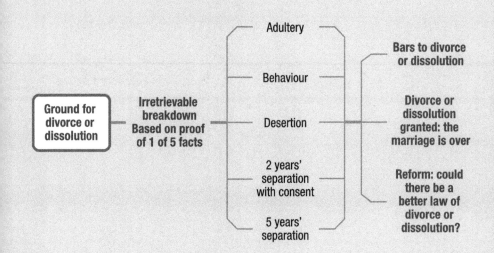

■ Introduction

Divorce is the legal death of the marriage.

A marriage is brought to an end by the death of either spouse or a decree of divorce issued by the courts. It is only possible to petition for a divorce after one year of marriage. The law on divorce is set out in Part 1 of the Matrimonial Causes Act 1973. The party who wants to end the marriage can apply to the court for a divorce. That party is known as the petitioner. The other party, the respondent, can either accept that the marriage has come to an end or seek to defend the divorce. The 1973 Act, in section 1(2), sets down a single ground for divorce: that the marriage has broken down irretrievably. However, it is only possible to prove that by establishing one of the 'five facts'. Even if the ground for divorce is made out, there are very limited circumstances in which the courts may still refuse to grant a divorce. These are known as the 'bars' to divorce. Many people believe that the current law on divorce is unsatisfactory and needs to be reformed. The law on dissolution of civil partnerships is very similar to that of divorce for marriages.

ASSESSMENT ADVICE

Essay questions

Essay questions on divorce tend to ask you to discuss the current law on divorce. You will need to explain the ground for divorce and examine the five facts. Don't forget also to consider the bars to divorce. Sometimes essay questions ask whether or not the law on divorce should be reformed. You will then need to discuss some of the problems with the current law and consider how they could be dealt with by changing the law.

Problem questions

Problem questions often raise issues about the meaning of the five facts. Particularly popular are questions concerning the meaning of adultery, unreasonable behaviour or separation. Sometimes the case may raise the issue of a possible bar to divorce.

■ Sample question

Could you answer this question? Below is a typical problem question that could arise on this topic. Guidelines on answering the question are included at the end of this chapter; a sample essay question and guidance on tackling it can be found on the companion website.

PROBLEM QUESTION

Fiona and George have been married for five years. For the past two years they have lived in the same house, but have had separate bedrooms, although Fiona still cooks meals for them both and George washes their clothes. They have not spoken a word to each other for nearly a year. Several weeks ago Fiona admitted that she spent the night with another man. George has decided he wants a divorce; Fiona does not. George is very rich; Fiona is very poor.

Discuss whether George is entitled to a divorce.

■ The ground for divorce

KEY DEFINITION: Ground for divorce

The ground for divorce is that the marriage has broken down irretrievably. But that can only be proved by showing one of the 'five facts'.

The **ground for divorce** is that the marriage has broken down irretrievably. But this can only be proved by showing one of the five facts. If it is not possible to show one of the facts, then a divorce cannot be granted, even if in fact the marriage has broken down. Also, even if one of the facts is demonstrated, the court could decide that the marriage has not broken down irretrievably (section 1(4), Matrimonial Causes Act 1973). But that would be very rare.

Irretrievable breakdown ———————— *None of the 5 facts proved* ———————— No divorce possible

No irretrievable breakdown ———————— *One of the 5 facts proved* ———————— No divorce possible

Irretrievable breakdown ———————— *One of the 5 facts proved* ———————— Divorce possible

Buffery v *Buffery* [1988] 2 FLR 365 (CA)

Concerning: the ground for divorce

Facts

It was found by the judge that the marriage had irretrievably broken down. The couple had nothing in common, never went out and were unable to communicate with each other. However, none of the five facts could be made out.

Legal principle

A divorce could not be granted. Even if the marriage had broken down irretrievably, a divorce could only be granted where one of the five facts was made out. The couple would have to separate for two years in order to get a divorce.

✎ **EXAM TIP**

A common error is to state that one of the facts is a ground for divorce:

WRONG: Desertion is a ground for divorce.

RIGHT: Desertion is one of the facts from which the court can conclude that the marriage has broken down irretrievably, which is the ground for divorce.

▆ Adultery

The **adultery** fact that can prove the ground for divorce is found in section 1(2)(a), MCA 1973. Sexual activity between same-sex couples will not amount to adultery.

KEY STATUTE

Matrimonial Causes Act 1973, section 1(2)(a)

'[. . .] that the respondent has committed adultery and the petitioner finds it intolerable to live with the respondent.'

KEY DEFINITION: Adultery

Adultery is voluntary sexual intercourse between a man and a woman, one or both of whom is married. Sexual intimacy short of sexual intercourse will not amount to adultery.

In order to rely on the adultery fact, it is necessary to show two things:

- the respondent has committed adultery;
- the petitioner finds it intolerable to live with the respondent.

Note also that you cannot rely on your own adultery to base a divorce petition! Under section 2(1), Matrimonial Causes Act 1973 you cannot rely on the adultery ground if after discovering your spouse's adultery you have lived together for more than six months.

> **KEY CASE**
>
> *Cleary* v *Cleary* **[1974] 1 WLR 73 (CA)**
>
> *Concerning: the adultery fact*
>
> **Facts**
>
> The wife committed adultery. The husband forgave her and they were reconciled. However, this was short-lived and the wife left the husband again. The husband then petitioned for divorce.
>
> **Legal principle**
>
> The Court of Appeal accepted that there was adultery and that following the wife's conduct during the unsuccessful attempt at reconciliation the husband found it intolerable to live with her. A divorce was available, therefore, on the adultery fact.

> **✎ EXAM TIP**
>
> Remember that it does not need to be shown that the petitioner finds it intolerable to live with the respondent because of the adultery. This issue often arises in a problem question. A husband who does not care about his wife's adultery can still use the adultery fact if he could point to other things about her that mean he finds it intolerable to live with her. You should note, however, that if the couple have lived together for a total of six months after the petitioner discovered the adultery, then the adultery fact cannot be relied upon (section 2(1), Matrimonial Causes Act 1973).

■ Behaviour

The 'behaviour' fact is found in section 1(2)(b), Matrimonial Causes Act 1973.

> **KEY STATUTE**
>
> **Matrimonial Causes Act 1973, section 1(2)(b)**
>
> '[...] that the respondent has behaved in such a way that the petitioner cannot reasonably be expected to live with the respondent.'

This fact requires proof that the respondent behaved in a way that meant the petitioner could not reasonably be expected to live with the respondent. Notice that the question is about what can reasonably be expected of this particular petitioner. So, if a petitioner is particularly sensitive, then it may make it reasonable for her to be unable to live with the respondent. In *Livingstone-Stallard* v *Livingstone-Stallard* (1974) the court said the key question is: 'would any right-thinking person come to the conclusion that this husband has behaved in such a way that this wife cannot reasonably be expected to live with him?'

The following table gives some examples of what the courts have or have not found to be behaviour that demonstrated irretrievable breakdown.

Case	Facts
O'Neill v *O'Neill* (1975)	Husband was DIY fanatic who took eight months to replace toilet door: BEHAVIOUR FACT DEMONSTRATED
Pheasant v *Pheasant* (1972)	Wife never engaged in spontaneous displays of affection: BEHAVIOUR FACT NOT DEMONSTRATED
Lines v *Lines* (1963)	Husband required wife to tickle his feet for hours every evening: BEHAVIOUR FACT DEMONSTRATED

Under section 2(2), Matrimonial Causes Act 1973, if the couple have lived together for over six months after the final incident of behaviour relied upon in the petition, then that fact can be taken into account in deciding whether the behaviour meant that the petitioner could not live with the respondent. However, if the period of time was less than six months, the court should ignore it.

KEY CASE

Birch v *Birch* [1992] 1 FLR 564 (CA)

Concerning: the unreasonable behaviour fact

Facts

The husband was found by the court to be dogmatic, nationalistic and dictatorial. The trial judge had taken the view that the husband had not behaved so badly that a reasonable person could not live with him.

Legal principle

The Court of Appeal said that the correct question was: 'could this wife (who was particularly sensitive and passive) reasonably be expected to live with her husband?' It thought not and granted the divorce petition on the unreasonable behaviour fact.

! Don't be tempted to . . .

Blameless behaviour

An issue that has troubled the courts is whether the behaviour fact can be relied upon if the respondent is not at fault. The issue is raised particularly where the behaviour is caused by a medical condition. On the one hand, it might be thought harsh on a spouse to be divorced based on behaviour over which they had no control. On the other, the courts are aware that caring for an ill spouse can be an enormous burden. In *Katz* v *Katz* (1972) a wife was able to get a divorce from a husband who suffered from manic depression, whose behaviour was concerning and greatly disturbed the wife.

Desertion

KEY STATUTE

Matrimonial Causes Act 1973, section 1(2)(c)

'[. . .] that the respondent has deserted the petitioner for a continuous period of at least two years immediately preceding the presentation of the petition.'

This defines the 'desertion' fact. To amount to desertion, there must be actual **separation**, for no good reason and without the consent of the petitioner. To rely on desertion, the following must be shown:

- separation for at least two years;
- an intention by the respondent to desert the petitioner;
- no consent by the petitioner to the desertion;
- no just cause to the desertion.

✎ EXAM TIP

Watch out for a possible trap in a problem question. Normally you cannot rely on your own desertion. But a divorce is available in cases of so-called **constructive desertion**. This is where the respondent has behaved so badly that the petitioner has been forced to leave the home, leading to a separation between the parties. In all cases of constructive desertion the behaviour ground is available and so the notion is of little practical relevance.

Two years' separation

KEY STATUTE

Matrimonial Causes Act 1973, section 1(2)(d)

'[. . .] that the parties to the marriage have lived apart for a continuous period of at least two years immediately preceding the presentation of the petition . . . and the respondent consents to a decree being granted.'

Section 1(2)(d) defines the 'two-year separation' fact. To rely on this fact it must be shown that the parties have lived apart for two years AND that the respondent consents to the divorce. If the respondent does not consent, the petitioner must rely on the five-year separation fact. That could be a long wait.

KEY DEFINITION: Separation

Separation requires the parties to live in separate households. Normally this will be in separate houses, but it is possible for them to live separate lives under the same roof. The court will consider whether or not they were sharing communal living (e.g. were they eating together; engaging in household tasks together). As well as living separately at least one of the parties must have reached the conclusion that the marriage is at an end (*Santos* v *Santos* (1972)).

Five years' separation

KEY STATUTE

Matrimonial Causes Act 1973, section 1(2)(e)

'[. . .] that the parties to the marriage have lived apart for a continuous period of at least five years immediately preceding the presentation of the petition.'

Section 1(2)(e) defines the 'five-year' fact. This fact requires proof that the parties have lived apart for five years. There is no need to show that the respondent consents. If a wife wishes to divorce her husband who does not want a divorce and who has behaved 'perfectly', this is the only fact she could rely on.

▄ Bars to divorce

Even if one of the facts is proved and the court concludes that the marriage has irretrievably broken down, the court may still not order a divorce if one of the bars applies. You will need to learn these bars to divorce for the exam. They are as follows.

- Section 3(1), MCA states that it is not possible to petition for a divorce until you have been married for one year. The only option for a spouse who has been married for a very short time who wishes to end the marriage is to have the marriage annulled or seek a judicial separation.

- Section 5, MCA provides a bar but this can only be used in cases based on the five years' separation. The court has the power to refuse to grant the divorce if two things are shown. First, that the respondent will suffer grave financial or other hardship if the divorce is granted (*Evans* v *Evans* (2012)). Second, that it would be wrong in all the circumstances to grant the divorce. The defence is rarely raised successfully.

- Section 12A, MCA enables a court to make an order which means that a divorce will only be granted once the couple have confirmed they have arranged for their marriage to be dissolved in the eyes of their religion. If one party refuses to allow the religious divorce, the court might refuse to allow the legal divorce.

- Section 10(2), MCA provides a bar that can be raised by a respondent but only for cases relying on two or five years' separation after the decree nisi. The court can only grant a divorce if it decides that financial arrangements for the petitioner are reasonable and fair, or the best that can be made in the circumstances.

- Section 41, MCA allows a court not to make a decree of divorce absolute if there are exceptional circumstances that mean that a court might want to make an order in respect of the couple's children but needs further consideration of the case.

✎ EXAM TIP

When considering the bars based on financial hardship, don't forget the extensive powers the courts have to redistribute a couple's property on divorce (see Chapter 5). It is unlikely that a court will not find a way of avoiding grave hardship by ordering maintenance payments or making some other financial order.

The harsh truth is that often on divorce both parties are going to be in a bad position financially. Dividing the limited resources between two people can mean that both are left in perilous circumstances. This means that relying on the section 5 bar often fails because, although on divorce the respondent may suffer financial hardship, it is not wrong to grant the divorce because there is nothing that can be done about it.

Procedure

So far we have looked at the law, but the practice of divorce is rather different from how it appears in the statute book. This is because of the 'special procedure' which was introduced in 1973. This means that in the case of an undefended divorce, there is no hearing at which the petitioner needs to prove the facts in the petition. In other words, the case is all decided on the paperwork. Cases of defended divorce are rare. They are expensive and unpopular with lawyers. Further, it is unheard of to get legal aid to defend a divorce. The sad truth is that if your spouse wants to divorce you, there is not much point in trying to get the courts to prevent it.

✓ Make your answer stand out

If an essay asks you to consider the current law, the examiner will be impressed if you can show a knowledge of how the law works in practice. Eekelaar *et al.* (2000) provide some very useful information on this.

Note, in particular, that in practice it is extremely rare for divorces to be defended. It is expensive and solicitors will seek to discourage it. Also note the negotiation that can go on between solicitors so that a petition that is acceptable to both sides can be presented to the court. This may not reflect the real reasons for the breakdown of the marriage, but the reasons the couple are willing to be aired in public.

Effects of divorce

On the granting of the decree absolute of divorce, the marriage is dissolved. One important consequence of this is that each party is now free to remarry. Another is that on divorce the financial orders often made during a divorce come into effect (see Chapter 5). Divorce also invalidates gifts and appointments to the spouse. However, divorce itself has no effect on the spouses' legal relationship with their children.

Reform of divorce

You should be aware of some of the key issues over reform of divorce law. These include the following:

- Should the law make it easy or hard to divorce?
- Should the law seek to discover whose fault it was the marriage ended?
- Should the parties be allowed or encouraged to blame each other?
- Should the law try to encourage divorcing couples to be reconciled? How?

In the table below, some of the main arguments for and against having a divorce system that requires or permits proof of fault will be discussed. Many commentators are convinced that we need to move to a system where parties are not permitted to blame each other for the end of the marriage.

Arguments in favour of fault-based divorce	Arguments in favour of no-fault divorce
It is a psychological need for parties to blame each other in divorce and the law should recognise this	The law should seek to minimise feelings of bitterness, not exacerbate them
If one party has behaved badly and caused the end of the marriage, that wrong should be publicly acknowledged	It is not really possible to ascertain who is to blame for ending a marriage
If it is too easy to divorce, marriage will become devalued	Forcing people to remain married who want to be divorced just because neither of them has behaved particularly badly is unjustifiable

The 1996 Family Law Act was passed, which was to create a new law on divorce; however, the divorce reform was never implemented. It would not have required the parties to make an allegation of fault against each other. It involved the parties divorcing over a period of at least a year. It sought to encourage the parties to be reconciled and to consider the use of mediation. The table below outlines the structure of the Act.

Minimum time from start of process	Action
0 months	The divorce process is initiated by one spouse attending an information meeting, which gives advice on various issues relating to divorce. After this the parties are meant to consider if they really want a divorce
3 months	One or both parties can file a statement of marital breakdown. There is no opportunity to allege fault
3 months 14 days	The period of 'reflection and consideration' starts. The parties should consider whether they truly want to divorce and, if they do, what arrangements there should be for the children and finances. They can mediate or consult solicitors
12 months 14 days	If they have no children, they can apply for a divorce order; the court must be satisfied that the arrangements for the finances have been resolved
18 months 14 days	Those with children (or where a spouse has applied for an extension of time) can now apply for divorce. The court must be satisfied that arrangements for the finances and children are in place

The 1996 Family Law Act as it relates to divorce was never implemented. The early pilot studies were found by the government to be a failure. The government has never fully explained why the reform was not implemented. Some of the issues it may well have been concerned about include:

■ The government hoped that couples would be persuaded at the information meeting to take up mediation, rather than seek a lawyer. The take-up rate for mediation was disappointing.

■ Many people found the information meetings of limited use. The information given was general and it did not relate specifically to their case.

■ Many commentators thought that having to wait a year and a half or more for a divorce was too long.

Since the reform of the divorce law in the 1996 Act was abandoned, there have been no signs of the government seeking to attempt reform again. However, the Family Justice Review in 2011 suggested that if both parties agree to a divorce they should be able to apply for and receive a divorce through an internet site.

✓ Make your answer stand out

Many essays ask about the reform of divorce law. It is useful to think about why the Act failed. Helen Reece (2003) saw the Act as an attempt to persuade people to 'divorce responsibly'. The Act showed a tension between giving people the freedom to end their legal relationship if they wished, while at the same time wanting them to make that decision in a thoughtful and careful way. Others have criticised the Act for seeking to tell people how to act; requiring people to act rationally and sensibly at a time when their emotions are running riot (see e.g. Eekelaar (1999)). Cynics have suggested that the government's main hope was that if many more people chose mediation rather than seeking the advice of lawyers, this would reduce the legal aid bill and save money.

▧ Dissolution of civil partnerships

The law on the dissolution of civil partnerships is virtually identical to the law on divorce. A civil partnership can be dissolved on proof that it has broken down irretrievably; however, that can only be shown by proof of one of four facts. These match the facts for divorce except there is no adultery fact. In the government's view, if there was sexual unfaithfulness, the behaviour ground could be relied upon. So the difference is probably of no practical significance.

▧ Putting it all together

Answer guidelines

See the problem question at the start of the chapter.

Approaching the question

You will want to start by setting out the ground for divorce and explaining the five facts.

Important points to include

- Adultery: Has there been adultery? Has intolerance been shown?
- Unreasonable behaviour: Can the silence be unreasonable behaviour?
- Separation: Can they be said to be living separately? But note that Fiona does not consent. If there is no consent, the five-year bar must apply.

✓ **Make your answer stand out**

- Don't forget to consider whether any of the bars apply.
- Use a good range of case law.

READ TO IMPRESS

Booth, P. (2004) Divorce, *Family Law* 617.

Cretney, S. (2003) Private Ordering and Divorce – How far can we go?, *Family Law* 399.

Deech, R. (2009) Divorce – A Disaster, *Family Law* 923.

Eekelaar, J. (1999) Family Law – Keeping Us 'On Message', *Child and Family Law Quarterly Review* 387.

Eekelaar, J., Maclean, M. and Beinart, J. (2000) *Family Lawyers.* Oxford: Hart.

Herring, J. (2012) Divorce, Internet Hubs and Stephen Cretney in R. Probert and C. Barton (eds), *Fifty Years in Family Law.* Cambridge: Intersentia.

Reece, H. (2003) *Divorcing Responsibly.* Oxford: Hart.

www.pearsoned.co.uk/lawexpress

Go online to access more revision support including quizzes to test your knowledge, sample questions with answer guidelines, podcasts you can download, and more!

Financial issues on divorce and dissolution

Revision checklist

Essential points you should know:

- [ ] The range of orders that can be made under the Matrimonial Causes Act 1973, or Children Act 1989 and Child Support Acts

- [ ] The factors taken into account in deciding what order to make

- [ ] *White* v *White* and the following case law on the 'yardstick' of equality

■ Topic map

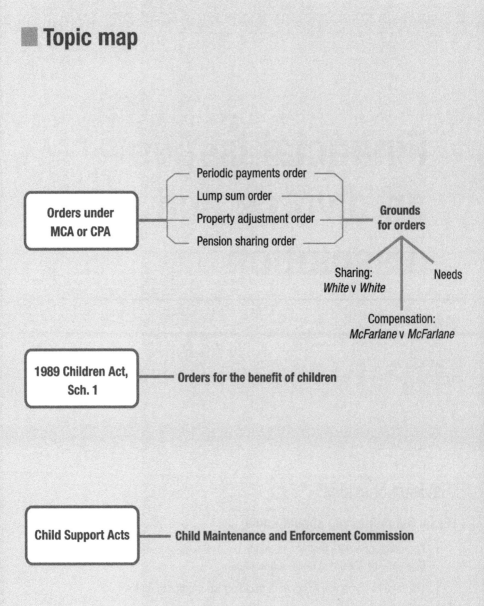

■ Introduction

Divorce can financially ruin you.

On divorce or dissolution of a civil partnership the court must divide the assets and income of the parties. The resources that used to support one household must now support two. Apart from the very rich, this is normally virtually impossible. Both parties will be far worse off financially after the divorce, although no doubt each will think the other has got a 'good deal'. The law's first concern will be with the children and to ensure they are adequately provided for, but even doing that has proved highly problematic.

Although in the reported cases there is much talk of the need to ensure there is fairness in this area, the problem is that there is no agreement about what fairness means! As Lord Nicholls (in *White* v *White* (2000)) admitted: 'Fairness, like beauty, lies in the eye of the beholder'.

ASSESSMENT ADVICE

Essay questions

Essay questions tend to ask you to discuss the way the courts make financial orders on divorce. You will need to discuss the range of orders available and the grounds for making the orders. Don't make the mistake of thinking that the leading cases such as *White* v *White* or *Miller* v *Miller* are representative: most couples are not fighting over millions. Indeed, for many couples there are more debts than assets. The 'big money' cases are interesting, however, because they highlight the theoretical issues surrounding financial redistribution. A good answer will bring in some of the academic commentary discussing the theoretical basis for the courts' powers. Essays can also appear on the troubled child support legislation. Here you can discuss why the child support system is in crisis and what might be done to sort out the mess.

Problem questions

Problem questions on this topic are likely to appear on the financial redistribution on divorce. They will require a good knowledge of the case law. Most of the case law has concerned very rich couples and so your problem question may well too. You will need a good understanding of *White* v *White* and *Miller* v *Miller*, *McFarlane* v *McFarlane* especially.

◼ Sample question

Could you answer this question? Below is a typical problem question that could arise on this topic. Guidelines on answering the question are included at the end of this chapter; a sample essay question and guidance on tackling it can be found on the companion website.

PROBLEM QUESTION

Alice and Bobby met while starring on the *Big Brother* TV show. They were both unemployed before the show and married shortly afterwards. They have been married seven years and are now divorcing. Alice has had a very successful career as a model, following the show, and she earns in excess of £2 million per annum. Bobby's father had given the couple £100,000 as a wedding present and they used this to launch Alice's career. Bobby, who is blind, has not been able to find a job and has no income. He looks after their baby girl, Charlene, born a year ago. They have agreed that Bobby will be Charlene's primary carer. The total assets, nearly all generated by Alice's career, are £1 million. They would have been more but Bobby is a 'shopaholic' who has spent many millions on expensive baubles. Experts suggest that, given her age, Alice will be able to continue her modelling career for the next three years, although it is unclear how her career will progress after that. Bobby has recently moved in with David and they are now living together. David is a wealthy man, although he has no intention of 'making an honest man' out of Bobby by entering a civil partnership with him. Consider what financial orders the courts may make on divorce.

◼ Orders for children

The law on periodic payments for children, originally set out in the Child Support Acts 1991 and 1995, has been reformed by the Child Maintenance and Other Payments Act 2008. It is highly complex. It is necessary to distinguish four categories of cases.

Order sought	Jurisdiction
Periodic payments for child of the payer	Child Support Agency; Child Support Act 1991
Lump sum orders for child of payer	The Courts; Children Act 1989, Sch. 1
Property orders for child of payer	The Courts; Children Act 1989, Sch. 1
Periodic payments for step-child or non-biological child of payer	The Courts; Matrimonial Causes Act 1973; Civil Partnership Act 2004; Children Act 1989, Sch. 1

Reform of Child Support

The government is reforming the law on child support. It hopes that most people will in the future reach their own agreements. Couples will be offered help to do this. The Child Maintenance Service will, for a fee, assist with the enforcement of agreements or help couples who cannot reach an agreement. The scheme will only apply to children who are under the age of 16 or in full-time education and where the child is not living with both parents.

✓ **Make your answer stand out**

A common essay question on child support asks how you think the law should be reformed. Should parents no longer be responsible for the financial support of their children and instead should the state undertake the role as primary financial supporter of children? Or is the lesson of the difficulties of the CSA such that we need to be much tougher with men who do not pay their child support? Is there a danger that if men have to pay too much child support they may decide to give up work or be unable to find another partner? These are all questions you should consider in an essay on reform of child support.

The Children Act 1989

Under section 15 of and Schedule 1 to the Children Act 1989, the court can make periodic payments or lump sum orders or property adjustment orders for the benefit of children. This Act applies to both married and unmarried couples. The significance of the provisions has been greatly reduced because the Child Support Acts now govern periodic payments for children. However, Schedule 1 is still useful where lump sum orders are needed to provide housing or other one-off items of expenditure. These tend to be in cases where the non-resident parent is very rich! In such cases children have been awarded houses, cars and furniture under this Schedule.

✎ **EXAM TIP**

Do not seek to use the Children Act 1989 in too broad a way. The courts have made it absolutely clear that they cannot order maintenance for a former cohabitee under Schedule 1, Children Act 1989. However, they can order the father to pay for the care of the child, and the mother can use this money, in effect, to pay herself for her child's care (*Re P (A Child: Financial Provision)* (2003)). Notice also under Schedule 1 that if a house is transferred to the mother for the child's benefit, it will revert to the father once the child is 18.

Child of the family

Watch out in a problem question for the position of step-parents. Where a spouse or civil partner has treated a child as 'a child of the family', he or she can be ordered under the Matrimonial Causes Act or the Children Act 1989 to support the child. This is so even if that party is not the child's biological parent. The orders that can be made and the grounds for making them are the same as those that apply to a married couple who are the parents of the child. But a person who has treated a child as a child of the family cannot be required to support that child under the Child Support Act 1991.

▣ Financial orders for spouses

The orders available

Under the Matrimonial Causes Act 1973 and Civil Partnership Act 2004 (CPA), the courts have wide powers to redistribute property between the spouses and to require ongoing financial support. The orders available are:

- Periodic payments order. This is an order that one spouse pays the other a certain sum of money each month (or week, or whatever is appropriate). The order can be fixed for a certain period of time: for example, for five years. The court can order that that period cannot be extended (section 28(1A), MCA); or allow the parties to apply to have the period extended if necessary.

- Lump sum order. This is an order that a fixed sum of money be paid by one spouse to another.

- Property adjustment order. This is an order requiring one spouse to transfer to the other all or part of an interest in a piece of property to the other. For example, a husband may be required to transfer the matrimonial home into the wife's name so that she and the children can live there.

- **Pension sharing order**. This is an order that involves splitting one spouse's pension so that it is shared between both.

KEY DEFINITION: Pension sharing order

A pension sharing order is an order that one party's pension be split at the time of the proceedings or thereafter. When the order comes into effect, the pension is split into two separate parts and they cease to be connected. This means, for example, that even if the husband dies, the wife can continue with her part of the pension.

✎ EXAM TIP

In a problem question, do not forget the requirement for the court to consider whether it is possible to make a clean break order. This is an order which terminates the ongoing financial obligations the spouses owe each other. Section 25A(1) requires the court to consider 'whether it would be appropriate so to exercise [its] powers that the financial obligations of each party towards the other will be terminated as soon after' the divorce as the court considers 'just and reasonable'.

Consider the arguments for and against making a clean break in the case before you.

The factors to be taken into account in deciding what order to make

When deciding what financial orders to make on the breakdown of a marriage or civil partnership, the court must consider the factors listed in section 25.

✎ EXAM TIP

When answering problem questions it is useful to consider the potential relevance of each of the factors listed in Matrimonial Causes Act 1973, section 25(2). When revising it is useful to learn at least one case to use for each of the different factors mentioned in section 25(2).

Factors listed in section 25	Example of relevance in case law
When the court is deciding what financial orders, if any, to make on divorce, the first consideration is 'the welfare while a minor of any child of the family who has not attained the age of eighteen' (s. 25(1))	In *B* v *B (Financial Provision)* (2002) all the assets of the couple were required to meet the needs of the child and the carer

Factors listed in section 25	Example of relevance in case law
'the income, earning capacity, property and other financial resources which each of the parties to the marriage has or is likely to have in the foreseeable future, including in the case of earning capacity any increase in that capacity which it would in the opinion of the court be reasonable to expect a party to the marriage to take steps to acquire' (s. 25(2)(a))	In *A* v *A (Financial Provision)* (1998) the court held that a 45-year-old mother with no employment record could not be expected to find full-time employment or start her own business
'the financial needs, obligations and responsibilities which each of the parties to the marriage has or is likely to have in the foreseeable future' (s. 25(2)(b))	In *S* v *S* (2001) it was suggested that obligations towards a second family could be taken into account, whereas in *H-J* v *H-J* (2002) it was held that as a matter of principle they should not
'the standard of living enjoyed by the family before the breakdown of the marriage' (s. 25(2)(c))	In *K* v *L* (2011) a couple had lived very simply, despite the wife having a share holding worth millions of pounds. It was held this was a good reason for not giving the husband half. In *Dart* v *Dart* (1997) it was said that in assessing a rich wife's needs the court would take into account the lifestyle she had enjoyed during the marriage
'the age of each party to the marriage and the duration of the marriage' (s. 25(2)(d))	In *Miller* v *Miller* (2006) the House of Lords suggested that in relation to short marriages of very rich couples, only marital assets would be divided in half. In longer marriages, all the spouse's property could be divided
'any physical or mental disability of either of the parties to the marriage' (s. 25(2)(e))	In *C* v *C (Financial Provision: Personal Damages)* (1996) after the divorce the severely disabled husband was left with £5 million, while the wife was left dependent on state benefits. He needed the money to meet his medical needs

Factors listed in section 25	Example of relevance in case law
'the contributions which each of the parties has made or is likely in the foreseeable future to make to the welfare of the family, including any contribution by looking after the home or caring for the family' (s. 25(2)(f))	In *White* v *White* (2000) it was held that contributions through home-making or child-caring were to be regarded as equal to those of the money earner. This led their Lordships to advocate a yardstick of equal division of assets unless there was a good reason not to
'the conduct of each of the parties, if that conduct is such that it would in the opinion of the court be inequitable to disregard it' (s. 25(2)(g))	In *H* v *H (Financial Relief: Attempted Murder as Conduct)* (2006) the husband attempted to murder the wife in front of the children. This conduct fell within section 25(2)(g)
'in the case of proceedings for divorce or nullity of marriage, the value to each of the parties to the marriage of any benefits which, by reason of the dissolution or annulment of the marriage, that party will lose the chance of acquiring' (s. 25(2)(h))	In *Martin-Dye* v *Martin-Dye* (2006) the Court of Appeal made a pension sharing order to ensure that the wife obtained a fair share of her husband's pension, to which otherwise she would not have been entitled

The 'big money' cases

In many cases the needs of the child and primary carer of the child dominate. Indeed, in most cases there is not even enough money to meet them. They, therefore, do not tend to raise controversial issues surrounding financial orders. It is the big money cases, where there are more than enough assets to meet the parties' basic needs, that require the courts to consider the other factors in section 25. Three recent House of Lords cases now dominate this area: *White* v *White* and *Miller* v *Miller*; *McFarlane* v *McFarlane*.

KEY CASE

White v *White* [2000] 3 FCR 555 (HL)

Concerning: financial orders in cases of rich couples

Facts

The Whites had assets of roughly £4.5 million when their marriage ended after 33 years together. Mr White had run farms and Mrs White had assisted in the business and raised the children. ▶

Legal principle

The primary objective in *ancillary relief cases* is to achieve fairness. The court must first meet the needs of the parties. If the assets exceed the needs of the parties, the court must consider all of the factors in section 25(2) and, in particular, the contributions of the parties. When considering those, there was to be no bias in favour of a money-maker and against the interests of a home-maker or child-carer. Indeed, where assets exceeded needs, there needed to be a good reason to justify departing from the 'yardstick of equality'. In this case there was a good reason to give Mr White a little over 50%, and that was that his family had provided them with an important sum of money to start their farming business.

KEY CASE

Miller v *Miller; McFarlane* v *McFarlane* [2006] 2 FCR 213 (HL)

Concerning: financial orders in big money cases

Facts

Miller v *Miller* involved a marriage that had lasted just under three years. The marriage ended when the husband had a relationship with a younger woman. At the date of divorce the husband was worth over £17 million, a significant portion of which he had earned during the short marriage.

McFarlane v *McFarlane* involved a marriage of over 16 years producing three children. When they met both husband and wife had been pursuing successful careers. However, during the marriage the wife had given up her job to care for the children and the house. She had not been employed for the vast majority of the marriage. They had assets of around £3 million, while the husband earned at least £750,000 per year.

Legal principle

In *Miller* the House of Lords, disagreeing with the Court of Appeal, held that the conduct of the husband in leaving the wife early in the marriage was not conduct that it was inequitable to disregard and, therefore, was irrelevant in the financial matters. Further, the fact emphasised by the Court of Appeal that the wife was led by the husband to reasonably expect a substantial award was irrelevant. However, the wife was entitled to a half share of the property generated during the marriage. This was calculated at £5 million.

In *McFarlane* it was held that simply dividing the capital of £3 million would not produce fairness. This could only be met by requiring the husband to make substantial periodic payments to the wife, although in the future the court would consider whether or not to continue the order. The periodic payments were needed to ensure that the wife received a fair share to mark her contribution to the marriage and to compensate her for the losses she suffered as a result of the marriage, by giving up her job.

! Don't be tempted to . . .

Interpreting *Miller*

There is an important difference between the speeches of Lord Nicholls and Baroness Hale in the *Miller/McFarlane* decision. You should explain and discuss this in an essay on ancillary relief. It concerns a case where the court has decided to divide the property generated during the marriage. Baroness Hale suggests that 'family assets' should be divided. These are the money earned by either party and their home and its contents. It would not include gifts or inheritances or 'business or investment assets generated solely or mainly by the efforts of one party'. Lord Nicholls suggests 'matrimonial assets' should be divided. He seems to have a wider understanding of this than Baroness Hale, including all property created by the parties during the marriage except gifts or inheritances. It seems that more law lords supported Baroness Hale than Lord Nicholls. If the lower courts follow Baroness Hale's approach (as they did in *Charman* v *Charman* (2007)), it will be necessary to ascertain how and to what extent a home-maker or child-carer can be said to have helped generate the money-maker's assets. It seems they could always show that they helped the money-maker in relation to the salary earned in a job, but perhaps not in relation to some business venture about which they knew nothing.

From *White* and *Miller/McFarlane* and subsequent case law we learn a number of important points of general application, including the following:

- Fairness is the guiding criterion for making orders under the MCA.

- There are three main theoretical grounds for making orders under the MCA: need, compensation and sharing the products of the marriage.

- There should be no discrimination between the contributions of a money-earner and a child-carer or home-maker.

- Although the court should consider making a clean-break order, this should not be at the expense of fairness.

- In a 'big money' case, the court should divide equally the economic products of the marriage unless there is a good reason not to. In a long marriage, the court will normally divide all the assets the couple has.

- If someone has deliberately hidden assets within a company in order to defeat a spouse's divorce claim the money can be taken from the company (*Petrodel* v *Prest* (2013)).

- Exactly the same principles apply whether the couple are opposite sex or same sex (*Lawrence* v *Gallagher* (2012)).

- In 'big money' cases, the yardstick of equality can be departed from if there is a good reason for doing so (see the following table).

Reason for departing from equality	Example of case where used
The money-maker had made an outstanding contribution to the marriage through an exceptionally successful career	*Sorrell* v *Sorrell (2005)*
The husband's family had assisted the couple financially	*White* v *White (2000)*
The needs of the children and their carer	*B* v *B (Financial Provision) (2002)*
There was difficulty in liquidating the assets	*A* v *A (2006)*
The couple set to one side money the wife had inherited	*K* v *L (2011)*
The wife had won money on the national lottery	*S* v *AG (2011)*

These principles were applied in the following cases.

KEY CASE

Charman v *Charman* [2007] EWCA Civ 503 (CA)

Concerning: financial orders for wealthy couples

Facts

The couple had been married for 28 years when they divorced. The husband had been very successful in business and generated £131 million. The trial judge awarded the wife £48 million and the husband appealed.

Legal principle

The Court of Appeal, following *Miller/McFarlane,* confirmed that all the assets a couple had were available for distribution. Where, however, the asset had been owned before the marriage or was a gift or inheritance, that might be a reason for departing from an equal division. In a long marriage, the basic principle was a division of all the assets, regardless of when they had been earned. In this case there should be a departure from equality due to the husband's outstanding business skills. The trial judge's order had been appropriate.

KEY CASE

McCartney v *Mills McCartney* [2008] FCR 707

Concerning: financial orders for short marriages

Facts

This is one of the most notorious divorces of the decade. Paul McCartney married Heather Mills in 2002 and divorced four years later. They had one child together. McCartney's wealth was estimated to be about £400 million.

Legal principle

The marriage was a short one and so following *Miller*, Bennett J held the court should share the 'marital aquest' (the property earned by the couple during the marriage). However, during the marriage no substantial sums of money had been generated. McCartney had given up work to enjoy married life. So there was no award on that basis. Nor was there any award based on compensation as Mills had not suffered any economic disadvantage as a result of marriage. The only award that could be made was that needed to meet her needs. McCartney was ordered to pay £16.5 million to meet the needs of his wife and daughter.

Pre-nups

Much controversy has surrounded the issue of whether the courts should give effect to pre-nups (sometimes called pre-marriage contracts or ante-nuptial agreements). These are contracts entered into by a couple shortly before they marry that seek to fix what will happen to their property in the event of a divorce. Traditionally the courts were reluctant to enforce these because they were seen as contrary to public policy. However, in the following case the courts indicated a change in attitude.

KEY CASE

Radmacher v *Granatino* [2010] UKSC 42

Concerning: The legal significance of a pre-marriage contract

Facts

The couple were married in London in 1998. The husband was French and the wife German. The wife was a wealthy heiress. They signed a pre-marriage contract that stated in the event of a divorce neither party could claim property belonging to the other. They have two daughters, but separated after eight years. The central issue in the financial claims was the significance of the pre-nup.

Legal principle

The majority held '[t]he court should give effect to a nuptial agreement that is freely entered into by each party with a full appreciation of its implications unless in the circumstances prevailing it would not be fair to hold the parties to their agreement.' (para. 75) Lady Hale dissented, believing that to give effect to pre-nups would undermine the special status of marriage and would work against the interests of women.

✓ **Make your answer stand out**

Remember that *Radmacher* does not say that pre-nups will always be enforceable. A party can claim that the pre-nup was not properly entered into (e.g. there was not full disclosure; there was undue pressure); or that the agreement was unfair (e.g. it did not adequately provide for the children of the marriage). However a pre-nup can certainly be upheld, even if it gives a wife significantly less than half the assets (*Z* v *Z* (2011)).

Be aware of some of the academic commentary on the decision. Contrast George *et al.* (2011) who oppose the decision and Miles (2011) who is more sympathetic.

Variation and appeals against orders

Sometimes after a court order has been made there are unexpected events that cause one party to the marriage to feel that the financial order made is no longer fair. In such a case the applicant may seek to appeal against the making of the order or seek to vary the periodic payments order made. The leading case is *Barder* v *Barder*.

KEY CASE

Barder v *Barder* [1988] AC 20 (HL)

Concerning: when events after the making of an order permit an appeal to be granted

Facts

A property adjustment order was made requiring the husband to transfer the former matrimonial home into the wife's name. Five weeks later, the wife killed the children and committed suicide. The husband sought leave to appeal against the original order in the light of the subsequent events.

Legal principle

Where soon after the making of an order there is an event that undermines a fundamental assumption behind an order, leave to appeal can be granted out of time. In this case leave should be granted because the death of the wife and children meant that they no longer had housing needs, which were the basis of the court order. This event happened soon after the making of the order and it was likely that a new order would be made.

✓ **Make your answer stand out**

There has been much academic writing on the theoretic support for the making of financial orders on divorce, and discussion as to the correct basis of orders. Note, in particular, the arguments by Deech (1977) that maintenance should be abolished as it discourages women from being financially self-sufficient; Eekelaar (2006) that the home-making spouse should gradually earn a larger and larger percentage of the other spouse's assets as the years go on; Herring (2005) that we should focus on society's interests rather than seeking to achieve fairness between the parties; and the proposals of the Law Society (2003) that much more weight should be given to pre-marriage contracts. In *Radmacher* v *Granatino* (2010) the Court of Appeal agreed that weight should be attached to a pre-marriage contract, if it had been properly entered into. A judge might decide to follow a pre-marriage contract, unless there was a good reason not to. An excellent exam answer would consider some of these different theoretical approaches. Although note that the courts have refused to accept that there is an overarching theory behind their approach.

■ Putting it all together

Answer guidelines

See the problem question at the start of the chapter.

Approaching the question

In a problem question like this you will want to go through all of the factors listed in section 25(2). Remember that the interests of the children are the court's first consideration. So start by considering the child. Here periodic payments in order to help the child will be required. Remember that, assuming Bobby is not on benefits, they are free to reach whatever agreement they wish, but after one year either party can apply to have their case assessed by the CSA, and so the minimum that they are likely to agree is what the Child Support Act would require. This, then, is likely to be at 12% of Alice's salary. ▶

Important points to include

As to spousal support, you will want to consider each of the section 25 criteria. Some of the difficult points raised by this question are the following:

- Bobby has special needs due to his disability. In *Miller/McFarlane* Baroness Hale talked about compensation only being due to 'relationship-based disadvantage'. On the other hand, disability is specifically mentioned in (e).

- Can Bobby claim a share in Alice's earnings? He certainly can to meet his needs. But can he claim a share due to contributions to the marriage? This is unclear following *Miller; McFarlane*.

- If the court does make a periodic payment order, should this be limited in time? Is this a case where a clean break is not appropriate?

- Having considered all the factors, you should go through the list of orders that the court has available (periodic payments orders, lump sum orders, etc.) and recommend an appropriate set of orders. With periodic payments orders, don't forget to discuss whether they should be of fixed duration.

✓ Make your answer stand out

There are lots of issues to discuss. There are some that candidates may overlook:

- Is Bobby's conduct in being a shopaholic a factor to take into account under sub-section (g)? Although not seriously bad, it is conduct that has a direct financial effect on the couple's finances. Notice in *M* v *M (Ancillary Relief: Conduct)* (2006) that the husband's gambling was a factor to be taken into account.

- Can Alice claim that her modelling career is an outstanding contribution justifying a departure from the *White* v *White* yardstick of equality? Or does the contribution from Bobby's family justify a departure from equality in his favour?

- Does Bobby's cohabitation affect his claim? Note here that *Fleming* v *Fleming* (2004) makes it clear that the court should not equate cohabitation and marriage and hold that the cohabitation automatically terminates periodic payments. However, it may mean that his needs (at least while he is living with David) are less than they would be if he was living alone.

READ TO IMPRESS

Cook, E. (2007) *Miller/McFarlane*: Law in Search of Discrimination, *Child and Family Law Quarterly* 98.

Deech, R. (1977) The Principles of Maintenance, *Family Law* 229.

Diduck, A. (2010) Public Norms and Private Lives: Rights, Fairness and Family Law, in Wallbank, J., Choudhry, S. and Herring, J. (eds) *Rights, Gender and Family Law*. Abingdon: Routledge.

Eekelaar, J. (2006) Property and Financial Settlement on Divorce – Sharing and Compensating, *Family Law* 754.

George, R., Herring, J. and Harris, P. (2011) 127 *Law Quarterly Review* 335.

Herring, J. (2005) Why Financial Orders on Divorce Should Be Unfair, 19 *International Journal of Law, Policy and the Family* 218.

Miles, J. (2005) Principle or Pragmatism in Ancillary Relief: the Virtues of Flirting with Academic Theories and Other Jurisdictions, 19 *International Journal of Law, Policy and the Family* 242.

Miles, J. (2011) Marriage and Divorce in the Supreme Court and the Law Commission – For Love or Money, 74 *Modern Law Review* 430.

Wikeley, N. (2006) *Child Support: Law and Policy*. Oxford: Hart.

www.pearsoned.co.uk/lawexpress

Go online to access more revision support including quizzes to test your knowledge, sample questions with answer guidelines, podcasts you can download, and more!

Who is a parent?

6

■ Topic map

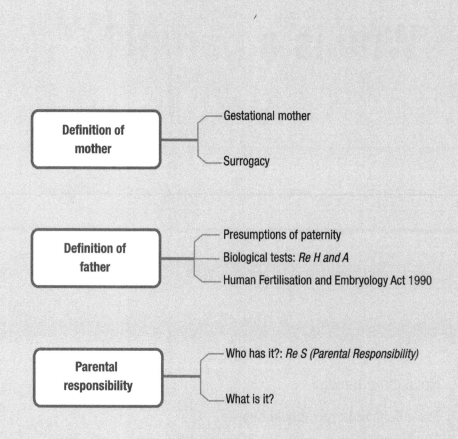

Definition of mother
- Gestational mother
- Surrogacy

Definition of father
- Presumptions of paternity
- Biological tests: *Re H and A*
- Human Fertilisation and Embryology Act 1990

Parental responsibility
- Who has it?: *Re S (Parental Responsibility)*
- What is it?

A printable version of this topic map is available from **www.pearsoned.co.uk/lawexpress**

■ Introduction

It used to be easy to define who a child's mother was and who a child's father was: not any longer.

With the advent of assisted reproduction and an increasing rate of parental separation, it is by no means guaranteed that a child will live with his or her genetic parents. This has made the definition of 'mother' and 'father' a complex question. Further, there is the crucial difference in law between being a parent and having parental responsibility. You can certainly be a father without parental responsibility, or have parental responsibility for a child but not be the child's mother or father. Running throughout this topic is a key theoretical question – who should be a child's parents: the genetic parents or those who are involved in the child's day-to-day care? It may be that we want to recognise both kinds of parents. Then we can end up with a child having, say, two fathers. But is there anything wrong with that?

ASSESSMENT ADVICE

Essay questions

Essay questions can take a variety of forms. An 'old chestnut' is to ask whether all unmarried fathers should get parental responsibility. This question, or a variant on it, is so popular that it is worth being familiar with the relevant case law and arguments. In this, and all essays on this topic, it is important to distinguish between the concepts of who is a parent and who has parental responsibility. Top-quality essays will discuss some of the theoretical issues about where parental rights come from and how they may assist in deciding who is a parent. This is especially useful in an essay that asks you to discuss the way the law allocates parenthood.

Problem questions

Problem questions are likely to centre on cases involving assisted reproduction or surrogacy. These will require a good knowledge of the relevant provisions of the Human Fertilisation and Embryology Acts 1990 and 2008 and the case law seeking to interpret that legislation. Problems are likely to require you to consider not only who is the parent of the child but also who, if anyone, has parental responsibility for the child.

■ Sample question

Could you answer this question? Below is a typical essay question that could arise on this topic. Guidelines on answering the question are included at the end of this chapter; a sample problem question and guidance on tackling it can be found on the companion website.

ESSAY QUESTION

Who gets parental responsibility for a child? Should all parents automatically be given parental responsibility?

■ Who are the parents of the child?

✎ EXAM TIP

Always keep the distinction between who is a parent and who has parental responsibility separate. In a problem question, first consider who are the child's mother and father, and then consider who has parental responsibility for the child. In an essay question, it is useful in the introduction to highlight this distinction, so keep it clear what you are discussing.

Who is the mother of the child?

Section 33 of the Human Fertilisation and Embryology Act 2008 makes it clear that it is the woman who gives birth who is the child's mother. This is so even if she is carrying an embryo using a donated egg. This also means that in a case of **surrogacy** the woman who gives birth is the mother.

KEY DEFINITION: Surrogacy

Under a surrogacy arrangement, a couple ('the commissioning couple') ask a woman ('the surrogate mother') to carry a child for them. The agreement is that shortly after birth the surrogate mother will hand the child to the commissioning couple for them to bring up. Sometimes the surrogate mother is a friend or relative of the commissioning couple; other times she is paid.

Who is the father of the child?

The simple answer is that the father is the genetic father of the child. But there is much more to the legal position than that. It is necessary first to consider the presumptions that the law uses in order to establish that a man is the genetic father of the child. Second, it is necessary to look at the Human Fertilisation and Embryology Act 1990, which deals with cases of **assisted reproduction**. This allows for some men who are not genetic fathers to be legal fathers of a child, and other men who are genetic fathers not to be the legal father.

Presumptions of paternity

In the following cases F is presumed to be the father of the child concerned:

- if F is married to the mother of the child at the time of the birth (the '*pater est*' presumption);
- if F is registered as the father of the child on the child's birth certificate;
- if circumstances are proved that strongly indicate that F is the father of the child (e.g. he was known to have spent the night with the mother at the time of conception).

In the absence of one of the presumptions, a man can only prove that he is the father of a child by applying to the court for biological tests to be carried out. Nowadays these are based on DNA. The court will order tests if that is in the best interests of the child. In recent cases they have normally ordered tests, arguing that it is important for a child to know who his or her genetic parents are (*Re H and A* (2002)). However, if it can be shown that doing tests will cause serious harm to the child, they will not be ordered (*J* v *C* (2007)).

The Human Fertilisation and Embryology Acts 1990 and 2008

This legislation governs assisted reproductive treatments in the UK. The statutes provide for two situations where a man who is not the **genetic father** of a child is nevertheless the child's legal father. You will need to make sure you have a clear understanding of these for the purposes of the exam.

The first is section 35 of the 2008 Act.

KEY STATUTE

Human Fertilisation and Embryology Act 2008, section 35

'If –

(a) at the time of the placing in her of the embryo or of the sperm and eggs or of her artificial insemination, W was a party to a marriage, and

(b) the creation of the embryo carried by her was not brought about with the sperm of the other party to the marriage,

then, subject to section 38(2) to (4), the other party to the marriage is to be treated as the father of the child unless it is shown that he did not consent to the placing in her of the embryo or the sperm and eggs or to her artificial insemination (as the case may be).'

This provision means that if a married woman receives assisted reproductive treatment at a **licensed clinic**, her husband will be the father of the child born, unless he did not consent. This is so even if donated sperm is used and, therefore, he is not the genetic father. In such a case the sperm donor will not be the father of the child born (s. 41). Note: this provision only applies to treatment in a licensed clinic. It would not apply if a wife asked a friend for some sperm and used it to inseminate herself. In that case, the friend would be the father.

Note that section 35 also applies if a woman is in a civil partnership with another woman. In that case the partner will be a parent of the child. Rather oddly, she is not described as the mother, but will be treated as the 'other parent'.

The second provision by which a man can be the father of a child to whom he is not genetically related is if the child is born following assisted reproductive services at a licensed clinic and the agreed parenthood conditions are satisfied. These are as follows.

KEY STATUTE

Human Fertilisation and Embryology Act 2008, section 37

1. The agreed fatherhood conditions referred to in section 36(b) are met in relation to a man ("M") in relation to treatment provided to W under a licence if, but only if –

   (a) M has given the person responsible a notice stating that he consents to being treated as the father of any child resulting from treatment provided to W under the licence,

   (b) W has given the person responsible a notice stating that she consents to M being so treated,

   (c) neither M nor W has, since giving notice under paragraph (a) or (b), given the person responsible notice of the withdrawal of M's or W's consent to M being so treated,

   (d) W has not, since the giving of the notice under paragraph (b), given the person responsible –

       (i) a further notice under that paragraph stating that she consents to another man being treated as the father of any resulting child, or

       (ii) a notice under section 44(1)(b) stating that she consents to a woman being treated as a parent of any resulting child, and

   (e) W and M are not within prohibited degrees of relationship in relation to each other.'

In short this means that if a woman receives licensed treatment, and has agreed that a man shall be the father of the child and he has agreed to that, then he shall be the father in the eyes of the law. The agreed parenthood provisions can also apply to a female partner of a woman.

As already indicated, if a man donates sperm to a licensed clinic and his sperm is used by that clinic in the treatment of infertility in line with his consent, he will not be the father of any child born. However, since the Human Fertilisation and Embryology Authority (Disclosure of Donor Information) Regulations 2004 a child born after the regulations come into effect will be able to ascertain who the donor father was and some information about him.

✎ EXAM TIP

The Human Fertilisation and Embryology Authority (Disclosure of Donor Information) Regulations 2004 were passed to acknowledge children's rights to know their genetic parentage. Knowing who their genetic parents are is an important part of some people's sense of identity. However, if this issue comes up in an exam question, you should point out that there is no obligation on parents to tell children that they were born using donated sperm. So for children whose parents do not tell them, this new right is not worth the paper it is written on. Further, note that children born naturally have no right to know who their genetic father is. The mother is not required to name the father on the birth certificate, Although under the Welfare Reform Act 2009, a mother is expected to name the father.

It is important to remember that the basic legal position is that the genetic father is the legal father, unless there is a statutory provision declaring otherwise. That became a key point in the following decision.

KEY CASE

A v *Leeds Teaching Hospital NHS Trust* **[2004] 3 FCR 324 (HC)**

Concerning: who are the parents of a child after a mix-up in an IVF clinic

Facts

Mr and Mrs A attended a clinic for infertility treatment. By mistake, Mrs A's eggs were fertilised by sperm from Mr B rather than Mr A. The resulting embryos were placed in Mrs A and twins were born. The court was asked to declare the identity of the father of the twins.

Legal principle

Mr A could not be a father based on section 28(2) HFE Act 1990 because he had not consented to the placing of this embryo (made using another man's sperm) into his wife. Nor could he be a father based on section 28(3) because, again, he had not consented to receive these treatment services (using another man's sperm) with the mother. In the absence of any statutory provision to the contrary, the genetic father is the legal father and so in this case Mr B was the child's father. However, Mr and Mrs A, if they wished, could adopt the child or Mr A could apply for parental responsibility. The availability of these legal mechanisms to formalise the situation meant there was not improper interference with the rights of Mr and Mrs A under Article 8, ECHR.

 Surrogacy

As we have already seen in a case of surrogacy, the surrogate mother (the mother who gives birth) will be the legal mother. However, under section 54 of the Human Fertilisation and Embryology Act 2008, the commissioning couple can apply for a parental order that will make them the parents of the child and will end the parental status of the mother. The requirements for obtaining a parental order are strict. They include that the couple must be married; that one of them is the genetic parent of the child; and that it is in the child's interests that the order be made. If it is not possible to apply for a parental order, the commissioning couple could seek to adopt the child or apply for a residence order. If there is a dispute over who should look after a child, the court will decide, on the basis of the welfare principle in section 1 of the Children Act 1989, who is best able to care for the child (*Re P (Surrogacy: Residence)* (2008)).

What is parental responsibility?

> **KEY STATUTE**
>
> **Children Act 1989, section 3(1)**
>
> 'In this Act "parental responsibility" means all the rights, duties, powers, responsibilities and authority which by law a parent of a child has in relation to the child and his property.'

Despite this fine-sounding definition of parental responsibility in the Children Act, in fact the concept is somewhat elusive. Surprisingly, it is far from clear what the rights and powers of a parent are. Here is a list of some of the rights a parent with parental responsibility has, although this is, no doubt, an incomplete list:

■ the right to make decisions about the child's education;

■ the right to 'possession' of the child – it is an offence to remove a child from a parent without lawful authority;

■ the right to choose a child's religion;

■ the right to consent to medical treatment for a child;

■ the right to consent to adoption (see Chapter 10);

■ the right to choose a child's name;

■ the right to apply for court orders in respect of the child.

These have never been set out in a statute or case law. Indeed, the essence of parental responsibility itself is ambiguous. Contrast the understanding of parental responsibility in these two important cases on the concept: *Re S (Parental Responsibility)* (1995) and *M* v *M (Parental Responsibility)* (1999).

KEY CASE

Re S (Parental Responsibility) **[1995] 2 FLR 648 (CA)**

Concerning: when an unmarried father should be given parental responsibility

Facts

The mother and father were unmarried but had cohabited and raised child S. They separated and the father sought contact with the child and a parental responsibility order. The mother opposed the application because the father had recently been convicted of possessing obscene paedophilic literature.

Legal principle

Parental responsibility was a status that acknowledged the man as a father of the child who was committed to her. When considering an application for parental responsibility, the court should remember that parental responsibility did not give a right to interfere in day-to-day matters, and if there were concerns about its misuse, orders under section 8 of the Children Act 1989 could restrict its use. The parental responsibility order would inform the child that her father cared for her. In this case the father should be granted parental responsibility as he had shown commitment and attachment to the child.

KEY CASE

M v *M (Parental Responsibility)* **[1999] 2 FLR 737 (FD)**

Concerning: when an unmarried father can be granted parental responsibility

Facts

The unmarried father of a child suffered from learning difficulties and his mental state was worsened by a motorcycle accident. This left him with severe brain damage and he was liable to violent outbursts. He applied for parental responsibility of the child.

Legal principle

His mental condition meant that he lacked the capacity to exercise the rights, responsibilities and duties associated with parental responsibility and so he should not be granted it, even though he demonstrated attachment and commitment to the child.

So, as is clear from these two cases, sometimes the courts have seen parental responsibility as no more than a confirmation that the man is a committed father of the child and in other cases it is seen as providing an important set of rights.

> **!** **Don't be tempted to . . .**
>
> **The duty to consult**
> Section 2(7) of the Children Act 1989 appears to suggest that a parent with parental responsibility can act alone and need not consult with anyone else. However, the courts have not interpreted the law in that way. They have said that over fundamental and important issues there should be consultation. They have not produced a definitive list but they include decisions over education: *Re G (Parental Responsibility: Education)* (1994); circumcision: *Re J (Specific Issue Orders: Child's Religious Upbringing and Circumcision)* (2000); and changing a child's name: *Dawson* v *Wearmouth* (1999). The conflict between the wording of the statute and the views of the courts is puzzling.

Who gets parental responsibility?

You will need to be able to explain clearly and accurately in the exam who in law is given parental responsibility. All mothers get parental responsibility automatically. Not all fathers do. There are some who get parental responsibility automatically. They are:

- all fathers married to the mother of the child;

- all fathers registered on the birth certificate of the child (section 4(1)(a), Children Act 1989) (although note that is only true of fathers registered after the Adoption and Children Act 2002 came into force).

If the father does not get parental responsibility automatically, he can take steps to acquire it in the following ways:

- He can enter a parental responsibility agreement with the mother (s. 4(1)(b)).

- He can apply for a parental responsibility order (s. 4(1)(c)).

- He can apply for a residence order from a court.

- He can apply to adopt the child.

If a father applies for parental responsibility the court will grant it to him if that is in the best interests of the child (*Re W (A child)* (2013)). If there is evidence that the father will misuse parental responsibility to harass the mother, that would be reason not to grant it to him (*Re M (A Child)* (2013)).

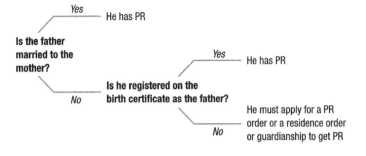

✓ Make your answer stand out

There is much academic writing on whether all fathers should get parental responsibility. To some it is simply discriminatory to assume that a mother automatically deserves parental responsibility, but not a father (see e.g. Bainham (2006)). Others argue that parental responsibility should be given to those who actively undertake care of the child. That is nearly always the mother and so the law reasonably presumes her to be entitled to parental responsibility, but the same assumption cannot be made in respect of a father (see e.g. Masson (2006)). One way of considering the arguments is to ask yourself this: which would be worse for a child – to have a worthy father who lacks parental responsibility or an unworthy father who has it?

Note that a non-parent can acquire parental responsibility. This will happen where a non-parent is granted a residence order. Some lesbian couples have successfully sought a parental responsibility order for the child of one of them so that they can share parental responsibility (see Smith (2006)).

■ Putting it all together

Answer guidelines

See the essay question at the start of the chapter.

Approaching the question

This essay is in two parts. Of course, it is important to deal with both aspects.

Important points to include

If you have revised well you should not have particular difficulty explaining who gets parental responsibility. In answering the second part you will want to discuss the following issues:

- What is parental responsibility? As we have already seen, it is far from clear what parental responsibility is and yet that is key if we are to decide who should get it.

- Is the law discriminatory? Note that the law draws a distinction between men and women and between married and unmarried fathers. Is this justifiable? (Note that the European Court of Human Rights in *B* v *UK* (2000) rejected an argument that the UK law was discriminatory.) Also consider whether the child may have a better argument of being discriminated against on the ground of illegitimacy.

- Should not the person who knows the child best make decisions for the child? That will be the resident parent (the mother normally). Is there not, therefore, a case for saying that after separation the resident parent alone should have parental responsibility?

- What do you make of the fact that many unmarried fathers are unaware that they lack parental responsibility (see Pickford (1999))? Should the law match people's expectations? Or does this research indicate that it does not really matter whether a person has parental responsibility or not?

✓ **Make your answer stand out**

We have to make generalisations in this area. However the law is structured, some parents who deserve parental responsibility will not get it automatically, and some parents who should not get it do get it automatically. Consider whether the current structure provides the best generalisation.

READ TO IMPRESS

Bainham, A. (2006) The Rights and Obligations Associated with the Birth of a Child, in Spencer, J. and du Bois-Pedain, A. (eds) *Freedom and Responsibility in Reproductive Choice*. Oxford: Hart.

Bainham, A. (2008) Arguments over Parentage, 67 *Cambridge Law Journal* 322.

Diduck, A. (2007) If only we can Find the Appropriate Terms to Use the Issue will be Solved: Law, Identity and Parenthood, *Child and Family Law Quarterly* 458.

Eekelaar, J. (1991) Parental Responsibility: State of Nature or Nature of the State?, 13 *Journal of Social Welfare and Family Law* 37.

Fortin, J. (2009) Children's Right to Know Their Origins – Too Far, Too Fast?, *Child and Family Law Quarterly* 37.

Gilmore, S. (2003) Parental Responsibility and the Unmarried Father – a New Dimension to the Debate, *Child and Family Law Quarterly* 21.

Masson, J. (2006) Parenting by Being; Parenting by Doing – in Search of Principles for Founding Families, in Spencer, J. and du Bois-Pedain, A. *Freedom and Responsibility in Reproductive Choice*. Oxford: Hart.

McCandless, J. and Sheldon, S. (2010) The Human Fertilisation and Embryology Act 2008 and the Tenacity of the Sexual Family Form, 73 *Modern Law Review* 175.

Pickford, R. (1999) Unmarried Fathers and the Law, in Bainham, A., Day Sclater, S. and Richards, M. (eds) *What is a Parent?* Oxford: Hart.

Probert, R., Gilmore, S. and Herring, J. (2009) *Responsible Parents and Parental Responsibility*. Oxford: Hart.

Smith, L. (2006) Is Three a Crowd? Lesbian Mothers' Perspectives on Parental Status, *Child and Family Law Quarterly* 231.

www.pearsoned.co.uk/lawexpress

Go online to access more revision support including quizzes to test your knowledge, sample questions with answer guidelines, podcasts you can download, and more!

Resolving disputes over children's upbringing

7

Revision checklist

Essential points you should know:

- [ ] The meaning and use of the welfare principle
- [ ] How the Human Rights Act interacts with the welfare principle
- [ ] The checklist of factors
- [ ] The law on residence and contact orders

■ Topic map

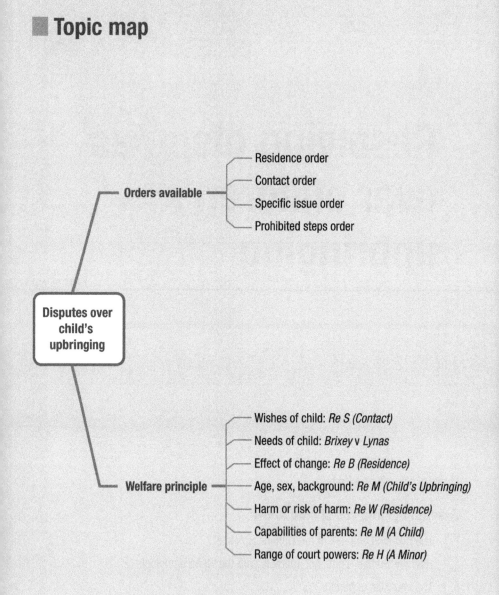

Orders available
- Residence order
- Contact order
- Specific issue order
- Prohibited steps order

Disputes over child's upbringing

Welfare principle
- Wishes of child: *Re S (Contact)*
- Needs of child: *Brixey* v *Lynas*
- Effect of change: *Re B (Residence)*
- Age, sex, background: *Re M (Child's Upbringing)*
- Harm or risk of harm: *Re W (Residence)*
- Capabilities of parents: *Re M (A Child)*
- Range of court powers: *Re H (A Minor)*

A printable version of this topic map is available from **www.pearsoned.co.uk/lawexpress**

■ Introduction

In disputes over children, the welfare of children should be the court's sole consideration.

That is easy to say, but hard to put into practice. In many cases it is far from clear what is in a child's best interests and the courts have been faced with some truly difficult cases. Attracting much attention at present is the law on contact. Fathers 4 Justice and other pressure groups claim that the law is anti-men and is denying fathers access to their children. On the other hand, women's groups claim that some men are using contact sessions to carry on being violent to mothers and children. The courts are stuck in the middle. Parliament has introduced the Children and Adoption Act 2006, which seeks to encourage couples to reach agreement over contact cases and avoid them coming to court. The classes and counselling it advocates do not seem to have lessened the anguish these cases cause.

ASSESSMENT ADVICE

Essay questions

Essay questions on this topic could deal with a wide range of issues. Some focus on the welfare principle and ask about its meaning and justification. There is a wealth of academic commentary that can be used to discuss the benefits and disadvantages of the welfare principle (see e.g. Herring (2005)). A good essay will also consider the potential impact of the Human Rights Act on the welfare principle. The courts have taken the line that approaches under the HRA and under the welfare principle produce the same results, but few academics agree (see Choudhry and Fenwick (2005)). In your essay you could be asked to consider who is right: the courts or the commentators? Another very popular topic for an essay question is to consider the law on contact. You should make sure you consider both the issue of when a contact order should be made and how, if at all, it should be enforced.

Problem questions

It can be difficult answering problem questions in this area because each case depends on its own special facts. Just because the court has made one kind of order in respect of a particular child in a particular family does not mean the same order would be made with a different child with different parents. However, a good answer will have a broad knowledge of the case law and seek to use it to indicate how the court may respond to the case. Especially in a case involving contact, it is worth considering how the court might enforce the order if it was made.

■ Sample question

Could you answer this question? Below is a typical problem question that could arise on this topic. Guidelines on answering the question are included at the end of this chapter; a sample essay question and guidance on tackling it can be found on the companion website.

PROBLEM QUESTION

Daisy and Emilia are partners. They wish to have children together and they attend a licensed fertility clinic together. Donated sperm is used to fertilise Emilia's egg, which is then placed in Daisy. Daisy subsequently gives birth to a baby boy, Fred. Emilia also wants to get pregnant and she advertises in the local newspaper for a man who is willing to donate his sperm. The Revd George, the local vicar, answers the advert and offers his sperm, which is used to make Emilia pregnant. Subsequently, Henry is born. Emilia makes it clear to Revd George that he is to have nothing to do with the child. Emilia and Daisy bring up Fred and Henry together, each playing a full role in the children's lives. Despite the agreement, the Revd George has seen Henry once a year, but Henry does not know who his father is.

Ten years later Emilia and Daisy decide to end their relationship after Emilia is violent towards Daisy. They both want to have residence of Fred and Henry. Henry says he wants to live with Daisy and does not want to see Emilia. Fred is not sure what he wants. The Revd George seeks a court order giving him weekly contact with Henry. Henry has become a regular attender at the local church and Revd George also seeks a court order to confirm that Henry should be raised in the Christian faith.

What orders should the court make?

✎ EXAM TIP

This topic is difficult to revise for because there is so much case law covering the area. Try to make sure you know at least one case for each of the areas that have come up. Remember also that the courts have said that each case depends on its own special facts. That said, the courts have created several presumptions that direct the courts' approach.

■ Section 8 orders under the Children Act 1989

Most cases of disputes in courts over children between individuals arise by way of an application for a section 8 order. There are four kinds of orders that can be made:

- Residence order. This determines where a child is to live. It is possible to make a joint residence order in which a child will spend a roughly equal amount of time with both parents (s. 11(4)).

- Contact order. This is an order that the resident parent allow someone (usually the non-resident parent) to contact the child. The contact is normally face to face but in a case of indirect contact it might be by means of phone, text or e-mail.

- Specific issue order. This is an order that something be done to a child. It might be an order for the child to attend a specific school, or to receive particular medical treatment.

- Prohibited steps order. This is an order that something not be done to a child. For example, it may forbid the child from being removed from the country, or stop the child from being circumcised.

When making one of these orders, the court can attach a condition to the order (s. 11(7)). These can be used to 'fine tune' the order. For example, it might provide that the handover point for a contact visit will be a McDonald's 'restaurant'.

The grounds for making an order

When the court is considering an application for a section 8 order, the starting point is the welfare principle.

KEY STATUTE

Children Act 1989, section 1(1)

'Where the court determines any question with respect to –

(a) the upbringing of a child; or

(b) the administration of a child's property or the application of any income arising from it,

the child's welfare shall be the court's paramount consideration.'

This principle means the courts must focus on what is best for child, not what a parent would want. In *Re C (A Child) (Indirect Contact)* (2012) a father, who was in prison, wanted to be sent a photograph of his child every year. The Court of Appeal refused to make the order. Although it would comfort the father, the order would not benefit the child.

The court must also take into account the '**no order principle**'.

KEY DEFINITION: No order principle

The no order principle is contained in section 1(5) of the Children Act 1989: the court should only make an order if doing so would be better than not making an order at all.

When considering the welfare of the child, there is a list of factors in section 1(3) that should be taken into account. These are listed in the following table with an example from the case law of the way the factor has been used.

Factor listed in section 1(3), CA 1989	Example of case discussing that factor
(a) the ascertainable wishes and feelings of the child concerned (considered in the light of his age and understanding)	In *Re S (Contact: Children's Views)* (2002) the views of a 16- and 14-year-old that they did not want to have contact with their father had to be respected
(b) his physical, emotional and educational needs	In *Brixey* v *Lynas* (1997) the House of Lords suggested that it was common sense that very young children were better brought up by their mother
(c) the likely effect on him of any change in his circumstances	In *Re B (Residence Order: Status Quo)* (1998) the trial judge was criticised for ordering a child's residence to be changed based on a speculative hope that the other parent would be better. Unless there is a good reason not to, the child should be left in his or her current residence
(d) his age, sex, background and any characteristics of his that the court considers relevant	In *Re M (Child's Upbringing)* (1996) a child born to Zulu parents was held to be better brought up by his Zulu parents, than by his white English foster mother: in part, because they would share his cultural heritage
(e) any harm that he has suffered or is at risk of suffering	In *Re W (Residence Order)* (1998) the Court of Appeal rejected an argument that the fact that the mother and her new partner were naturists who were often nude in front of the children caused the children harm. The benefits of naturism were an issue on which there was a range of reasonable views. It was not shown to be clearly harmful

Factor listed in section 1(3), CA 1989	Example of case discussing that factor
(f) how capable each of his parents – and any other person in relation to whom the court considers the question to be relevant – is of meeting his needs	In *Re M (A Child) (Contact: Parental Responsibility)* (2001) the court found that the father was not able to provide effective care for his disabled child and so he could not be granted a residence order
(g) the range of powers available to the court under this Act in the proceedings in question	In *Re H (A Minor) (Section 37 Direction)* (1993) parents of a baby handed her over to a couple of friends who, months later, sought a residence order. The court made a residence order but also an order (under s. 37, CA) that the local authority investigate how the children were faring

✎ EXAM TIP

Don't forget to consider the human rights angle to the issues. This is especially true of problem questions. One approach is first to apply the welfare principle to the issue in the problem question and then to consider whether making such an order would improperly interfere with the Convention rights of one of the parties.

✎ EXAM TIP

Students sometimes struggle with applying a human rights approach to a problem. The right that is most often relevant in a family law case is Article 8, and so we will use that by way of example. In respect of each individual, e.g. the child and each parent, consider the following:

1 Does the individual have a relevant right to respect for family life that falls within Article 8(1) in this case? If not, then the individual cannot make a human rights claim under Article 8.

2 Are there interests or rights of others or societal interests that justify an interference with that right as necessary under Article 8(2)? If there are, then the individual cannot make a human rights act claim. If there are not, the individual can.

3 If in a particular case there are two or more people who can validly assert rights under Article 8, the court must undertake the 'ultimate balancing exercise' and decide which right is more important.

Articles by Choudhry and Fenwick (2005) and Herring and Taylor (2006) discuss this further.

It is not possible here to discuss all the kinds of cases that could come up in an exam. But here are some of the issues that are particularly popular with examiners.

The natural parent presumption

At one time there was a presumption that the child is best brought up by her genetic parents. In *Re M (Child's Upbringing)* (1996) this led the Court of Appeal to order that a Zulu child who had spent most of his life with a white couple in England be returned to his biological parents in South Africa. Interestingly, press reports reveal that the child had to be brought back to England after a few weeks because he was so miserable. However, following two recent decisions of the House of Lords, it is clear that although the fact that one of the parties is a parent is a factor to take into account, at the end of the day the question for the courts is simply: what order will best promote the child's welfare.

KEY CASE

Re G (Children) [2006] 3 FCR 1 (HL)

Concerning: the resolution of a parenting dispute between a lesbian couple

Facts

C and G lived in a cohabiting lesbian relationship during which G gave birth to two children using donated sperm from a licensed clinic. The children were raised by C and G together. On separation, the children lived with G and had regular contact with C. However, in breach of a court order, G then removed the children to Cornwall and contact with C ceased. When the matter came before the court, the judge granted primary residence to C, with regular contact with G. G appealed and the case went to the House of Lords.

Legal principle

The House of Lords held that the lower courts had placed insufficient weight on the fact that G was the mother of the children because she had given birth to them. Children should not be removed from their parents unless there are good reasons for doing so. The children should remain with G and have regular contact with C. However, the House of Lords did indicate that if G continued to thwart contact between the children and C, a judge might decide to change the children's residence.

Re B (A Child) (Residence Order) [2010] 1 FCR 1 (HL)

Concerning: residence orders

Facts

B, aged 4, had been raised since birth by his grandparents because his parents were unable to care for him. The father had recently seen a significant improvement in his life circumstances and had now married. He applied for a residence order. The expert report stated that the grandparents were providing excellent care, but that the father could provide an adequate home for him. The judge in the family division made a residence order in favour of the father.

Legal principle

In residence cases the central legal principle was straightforward: the order should be made that best promoted the child's welfare. There was no right of parents to raise their children, even where they were able to provide an adequate level of care. In this case once it was determined that the child was well settled with the grandparents and that it would promote his welfare to remain with them, there was no alternative but to make a residence order in favour of the grandparents.

What weight should be attached to a child's views?

When thinking about the weight the court should give and does give to children's wishes in these cases, tie this in with the discussion about children's rights in Chapter 8.

As the table below shows, the courts have not been consistent in the weight to be attached to the child's views. I have a sneaking suspicion that if the judges agree with the children, they attach much weight to their views, but if they do not, they attach little weight. But that might be rather unfair.

Case	Reason for attaching or not attaching weight to the view of the child
Re M (Medical Treatment: Consent) (1999)	Where a child was refusing to consent to life-saving treatment, the court would not let the child 'martyr herself'
Re M (A Minor) (Family Proceedings: Affidavits) (1995)	The judge did not attach much weight to the views of a 12-year-old who wished to live with her father because he did not think she understood what life with him would really be like
Re S (Contact: Children's Views) (2002)	Children aged 16, 14 and 12 did not want to have contact with their father. Children of that age had to have their views respected. After all, the court could do nothing if they refused to see him
Re T (A Child: Contact) (2002)	If children are refusing to see their father, the court will only attach weight to that view if it is convinced that the view is genuinely their own and not 'imposed' on them by the mother
Re R (A Child) (Residence Order: Treatment of Child's Views) (2009)	The child was aged 10 and the judge should have given 'full and generous' weight to his views.

▦ When is a joint residence order appropriate?

You should be aware that there has been a notable change in the approach of the courts to joint residence cases. At one time it seemed that joint residence orders would only be appropriate in exceptional cases and those where there was no animosity between the parties. However, more recent cases indicate that they should not be regarded as exceptional, nor as necessarily inappropriate even if there is some bitterness between the parents, e.g. *Re R (Residence: Shared Care: Children's Views)* (2005); *Re K (A Child) (Shared Residence Order)* (2009). That said, such orders are still relatively rare – not least because they are only workable if both parents are living close to the children's school.

▦ Removal from the jurisdiction

Another issue that can arise in an exam is the removal of children from the jurisdiction. It is worth you revising the case law on this. If one parent wishes to remove a child from the jurisdiction, they require the leave of the court (s. 13, Children Act 1989). These cases are difficult. The resident parent wishes to start up a new life in a new country, or to return to her family and homeland; while the non-resident parent fears that if leave is granted they will lose all contact with their child. The leading case is *Payne* v *Payne* (2001) where the courts have emphasised that the welfare of the child is the paramount consideration (*Re L (Relocation: Shared Residence* (2012)). But, if refusing leave to the resident parent will cause them great distress, this will harm the child. Therefore, as long as the plans of the resident parent are reasonable, the court will normally grant leave. However, that principle will not be followed in cases where the care of the child is shared between both parties (*MK* v *CK* (2011)). Then it will be much harder to persuade the courts to grant leave. Some commentators argue that the courts are saying that they are promoting the welfare of the child, but are really protecting the rights of parents (contrast Hayes (2006) and Herring and Taylor (2006)).

▉ When should contact be ordered?

This is a hugely controversial issue and one that has attracted much media attention. In all the excitement it should not be forgotten that most couples are able to agree about contact arrangements between themselves and very few get to court. When they do go to court, in less than 1% of cases do courts refuse to order contact. The problem is not so much that the courts are refusing to grant fathers contact, but that the orders are so difficult to enforce.

First, there is the issue of when a court should make a contact order. The starting point is the welfare principle. The following is the leading case.

Note: the Court of Appeal is willing to confirm that there is an assumption that contact between a child and parent is beneficial (at least where they have an existing relationship) but not that there is a right of contact.

KEY CASE

Re L, V, M and H [2001] Fam 260 (CA)

Concerning: when it is appropriate to order contact in a case where there had been domestic violence

Facts

The Court of Appeal heard four cases. In each of them there was a history of domestic violence by the father towards the mother, and he was now seeking contact with their child. ▶

> **Legal principle**
>
> In all cases of contact the starting point was the welfare of the child. It would be wrong to say that there is a right for fathers to contact, or even a presumption that contact should be ordered. However, a court will be willing to make an assumption that contact between a child and a father is beneficial, although the strength of that assumption will depend on how well the child knows the father. In each case the court needs to weigh up the benefits and disadvantages of contact. In a case where there had been a history of domestic violence, there was no presumption against ordering contact but the court would be alert to the issues raised by expert psychologists of the dangers in ordering contact in such cases.

So decisions about contact should be made based on what is in the best interests of the child. There is no formal presumption in favour of contact (*Re W (Children)* (2012)), although it is very common for the courts to order some form of contact. The courts will normally want to enable some contact to take place between a parent and child, although in cases where there is clear evidence the contact will harm the child no contact will be ordered (e.g. *Re W (Children)* (2012) where the father was alcoholic and abusive).

The problem for the courts has been how to enforce these contact orders if the resident parent refuses to permit contact. Research suggests that this is commonly because the resident parent fears that the non-resident parent will be violent to her or the child. Presumably, these are fears the court has found to be ill-founded. The normal response in other areas of the law to a person who breaches a court order is that he or she should be imprisoned. But to do that in this situation will harm the child and probably be counterproductive. A child who sees her father apply for an order that her mother be sent to prison is unlikely to be keen on contact with him. Another option is to transfer residence to the father (*TB* v *DB* (2013); *Re S (Transfer of Residence)* (2011)).

The Children and Adoption Act 2006 inserts a new sections 11A–P into the Children Act which provide a range of orders the court can use that can include:

- A contact activity direction. This might require the parties to attend counselling or group sessions to encourage them to agree contact arrangements.

- A contact activity condition. These are used where a contact order has been made and the court hopes that an activity (such as counselling) will help contact to go ahead.

- Unpaid work requirement. The court will be able to impose on a resident parent who fails to make a child available for contact a requirement that they undertake unpaid work by way of punishment. (Note that because the non-resident parent cannot be ordered to have contact, he/she cannot be punished in this way for failing to turn up for a contact session.)

■ Compensation for financial loss. The court can require the resident parent to pay for losses the non-resident parent has incurred in preparation for the contact session (e.g. tickets to a theme park), if the resident parent fails to make the child available for contact without reasonable excuse.

Whether these will be effective remains to be seen.

✎ EXAM TIP

If you are facing an essay on contact, you should consider the approach the European Court of Human Rights has taken towards contact. If the non-resident parent is able to show that he or she has family life with the child, then that parent has a right of contact with the child under Article 8 of the ECHR (*Hokkanen* v *Finland* (1996)). However, that right can be interfered with if that is necessary in the interests of others, e.g. the child or the resident parent. If the state makes a contact order, it must take reasonable steps to enforce the order (*Glaser* v *UK* (2001)). Do you think the current law in the UK on contact is compliant with the Convention?

■ Putting it all together

Answer guidelines

See the problem question at the start of the chapter.

Approaching the question

The place to start with a problem like this is to be clear about who the parents of the child are.

Important points to include

Note that you will need to discuss section 27(1) to establish that Daisy is the mother of Fred. Fred has no father (if Emilia were a man she would have been the father). Emilia is the mother of Henry, and Revd George is his father (although DNA tests will be required to prove that).

▶

You will want to separate out the applications that are likely to be made to the court here. First, there will be conflicting applications from Emilia and Daisy for residence of Fred and Henry. Second, depending on the outcome of the residence applications, whoever does not obtain residence will seek a contact order. Third, there is Revd George's application for contact. Finally, Revd George might seek a specific issue order that Henry be brought up in the Christian faith.

You will want to start by explaining that the welfare principle will govern all the applications.

The key issues that will be raised are the following:

■ The importance of the 'natural parent presumption' as interpreted in *Re G (Children)* (2006) and *Re B (A Child) (Residence Order)* (2010).

■ The weight to be attached to the wishes of the child (see above).

■ The possibility of a joint residence order being made here. Note also the courts' preference for not separating siblings.

■ The significance to be attached to the domestic violence (see *Re L, V, M, and H* (2001)).

■ In relation to the application concerning religion, the courts are reluctant to order parents to raise a child in accordance with a religion and they will not want to be seen to favour one faith over another (*Re G (Children) (Religious Upbringing)* (2012)). It may be that the 'no order principle' is significant here: the child is at an age where he can make decisions about his faith and there is no real need for an order.

 Make your answer stand out

Consider the differences between *Re G (Children)* (2006) and *Re B (A Child)* (2010). Was there any difference in what the House of Lords was saying in these two cases?

READ TO IMPRESS

Bainham, A., Lindley, B., Richards, M. and Trinder, L. (eds) (2003) *Children and Their Families*. Oxford: Hart.

Choudhry, S. and Fenwick, H. (2005) Taking the Rights of Parents and Children Seriously: Confronting the Welfare Principle under the Human Rights Act, 25 *Oxford Journal of Legal Studies* 453.

Gilmore, S. (2006) Contact/Shared Residence and Child Well-Being: Research Evidence and Its Decisions for Legal Decision-Making, *International Journal of Law, Policy and the Family* 20.

Gilmore, S. (2008) Disputing Contact, *Child and Family Law Quarterly* 285.

Gilmore, S. (2010) Shared Residence: a Summary of the Courts' Guidance, *Family Law* 285.

Hayes, M. (2006) Relocation Cases: Is the Court of Appeal Applying the Correct Principles?, *Child and Family Law Quarterly* 351.

Herring, J. (2005) Farewell Welfare, 27 *Journal of Social Welfare and Family Law* 159.

Herring, J. and Taylor, R. (2006) Relocating Relocation, *Child and Family Law Quarterly* 517.

Herring, J. and Foster, C. (2012) Welfare Means Relationality, Virtue and Altruism, 32 *Oxford Journal of Legal Studies* 480.

Probert, R., Gilmore, S. and Herring, J. (2009) *Responsible Parents and Parental Responsibility*. Oxford: Hart.

Wallbank, J. (2010) (En)Gendering the Fusion of Rights and Responsibilities in the Law of Contact, in Wallbank, J., Choudhry, S. and Herring, J. (eds) *Rights, Gender and Family Law*. Abingdon: Routledge.

www.pearsoned.co.uk/lawexpress

Go online to access more revision support including quizzes to test your knowledge, sample questions with answer guidelines, podcasts you can download, and more!

Children's rights

Revision checklist

Essential points you should know:

- [ ] What is a right?
- [ ] The decision in *Gillick* and the resulting case law
- [ ] The role children play in court proceedings
- [ ] The relevance of children's wishes

■ Topic map

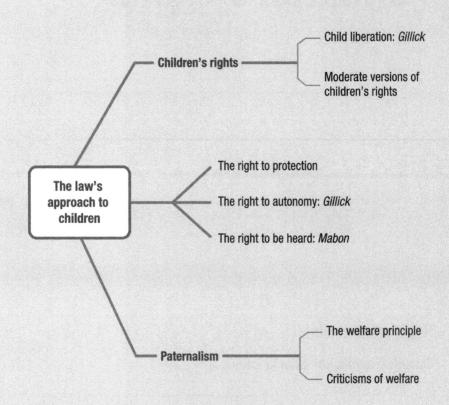

Children's rights
— Child liberation: *Gillick*
— Moderate versions of children's rights

The law's approach to children
— The right to protection
— The right to autonomy: *Gillick*
— The right to be heard: *Mabon*

Paternalism
— The welfare principle
— Criticisms of welfare

A printable version of this topic map is available from **www.pearsoned.co.uk/lawexpress**

■ Introduction

Do children have a right not to eat broccoli?

This is the kind of jokey question asked by those who think it absurd to talk about children having rights. However, the courts and many commentators do now talk in terms of children having human rights. After all, children are human. Most people, however, accept that children cannot have all the rights that adults have. This leaves the question of which rights children can or cannot have and that is an issue which has troubled the courts and commentators. The case law has mainly focused on the medical arena, with the crucial decision in *Gillick* finding that, if children have sufficient understanding on the relevant issue, they can give legally effective consent to receive medical treatment.

ASSESSMENT ADVICE

Essay questions

A typical essay question will ask whether the law recognises that children have rights and whether it should. When considering the actual law, it is important to appreciate that, although most of the cases have concerned the medical arena, their significance is much wider. A good essay may consider the extent to which these cases can be used in other areas where children's rights are relevant. It is also important to consider the different academic writings on whether children have rights and, if so, how they are to be understood. Try to keep your discussion of the theory grounded in concrete examples. Ask yourself: in what kind of cases will it matter what view I take of children's rights? Another important issue to consider when looking in an essay at children's rights is who enforces these rights? How easy is it for children to bring cases to court?

Problem questions

Problem questions in this area often centre around the *Gillick* decision and the case law applying it. You will need to be aware of the factors the court takes into account in deciding whether a child is *Gillick* competent. Further, what is the significance of being *Gillick* competent? A point that can be overlooked is that if a doctor is unsure how to proceed, she or he can apply to the court for guidance and the court will make the order based on what is in the best interests of the child.

Sample question

Could you answer this question? Below is a typical essay question that could arise on this topic. Guidelines on answering the question are included at the end of this chapter; a sample problem question and guidance on tackling it can be found on the companion website.

ESSAY QUESTION

Does the law recognise that children have rights? Should it?

What are rights?

KEY DEFINITION: Right

The concept of a right in law is much disputed and it is not possible to give a definition that would be universally agreed. When a person has a right to *x*, other people are bound by a duty to protect or promote the interests the person has in *x*. There need to be good reasons why the person should be prevented from *x*. A distinction can be drawn between an absolute right, in which case there are no circumstances in which the person can be denied *x*, and a conditional right, in which case if there is a good reason to interfere in the person's right, it cannot be enforced.

Do children have **rights**? This is a question that has troubled lawyers and philosophers for centuries. There is much dispute over the **jurisprudential** foundation of rights (see Read to impress). At one extreme are the so-called 'child liberationists' (or 'kiddie libbers') who argue that children should have all the rights that adults have. To many, to give children, for instance, the same rights in the area of sexual relations would leave them open to abuse and not liberate them. Most supporters of children's rights, therefore, argue that although children should have the right to make some decisions for themselves, there should be limits: children should not be able to make decisions that cause them lasting harm, for example.

Those who support children's rights are often critical of the main alternative approach to a rights perspective: one based on welfare. It is argued that such an approach leaves children open to having decisions made for them based on what adults think is best. History teaches us that these decisions often reflect the prejudices and misconceptions of adults, rather than being an accurate assessment of what is best for children. Now we can consider some of the benefits and disadvantages of a rights-based approach.

Advantages of a rights-based approach	Disadvantages of a rights-based approach
It respects children as people entitled to make decisions for themselves	Children have a 'right to a childhood' and should not have the responsibilities of adulthood imposed on them at a young age
History teaches us that adults do not in fact know what is best for children	Allowing children to make their own decisions can cause them serious harm and even restrict their ability to make decisions later in life
Rights offer a powerful legal tool to force the government and others to protect the interests of children	The values that should govern the law between parents and children should be based on love, care and mutual support, not individual rights

✎ EXAM TIP

When writing an essay on children's rights, you will want to draw out the distinction between those who emphasise children's rights, and those who are paternalists and emphasise children's welfare. Note, however, that for many issues in practice there is no difference which view you take. Children should receive adequate nourishment whether that is seen as a right or part of their welfare. Where the views tend to diverge would be a case where children want to do something that is harmful. From a straightforward paternalistic point of view, a child would not be permitted to do this, whereas a children's-rights perspective would let the children decide. Note, however, that sophisticated versions of paternalism agree that it is a good idea that children learn from their mistakes and that sophisticated versions of children's rights accept that children have rights of protection as well as rights to make decisions, and sometimes children should not be allowed to act as they wish. A good answer will demonstrate the complexity of the approaches.

■ Children's rights in the law

It was the decision of the House of Lords in *Gillick* that first indicated that the law might accept the idea that children can make decisions for themselves. You need to be able to discuss this case thoughtfully. It is worth reading the decision in full.

KEY CASE

Gillick v *West Norfolk and Wisbech Health Authority* [1986] AC 112 (HL)

Concerning: the consent of children to contraceptive advice and treatment

Facts

The Department of Health and Social Security issued a circular informing doctors that they would be acting lawfully if they prescribed contraception to girls under 16, even if they did not have parental consent. Mrs Gillick, a committed Roman Catholic with five daughters, sought a declaration that the circular was illegal.

Legal principle

The House of Lords held that parental rights existed in order to protect children. So the parental rights yielded to the rights of the child to make decisions for herself if she had sufficient understanding and intelligence. Therefore, a doctor can provide contraceptive advice and treatment to an under-16-year-old, without her parents' consent, if she has sufficient understanding of the issues involved and it is in her best interests to receive the treatment. The girl's consent would provide a defence to any crime or tort the doctor might be charged with.

The issue at the heart of *Gillick* came up again recently in *R (Axon)* v *Secretary of State for Health* (2006) in which Mrs Axon argued that if her under-16-year-old daughter wanted to have an abortion, she (Mrs Axon) should be consulted first. Silber J, following *Gillick*, held that a child under the age of 16, if competent, could consent to receiving an abortion and the doctor was not required to inform her parents. He explained that the law as set out in *Gillick* was not changed by the Human Rights Act. Indeed, rather surprisingly, he said that parents had no rights to family life in relation to a decision of their competent child in consenting to the procedure.

Although *Gillick* appeared to recognise that competent children have the right to make decisions about their medical treatment, it soon became clear that the law was not that straightforward, as the following case shows.

KEY CASE

Re R (A Minor) (Wardship: Medical Treatment) [1992] Fam 11 (CA)

Concerning: the consent of children to medical treatment

Facts

A 15-year-old girl had been placed in an adolescent psychiatric unit, suffering from mental illness. She refused to consent to psychiatric treatment, although her parents did. The experts explained that her mental state fluctuated wildly and although she might be competent at some moments, she would be incompetent at others.

Legal principle

A child whose mental state fluctuated between competent and incompetent was not *Gillick* competent. The court would order the treatment to be provided because that was in her best interests. Even if she had been competent and refused treatment, the doctors could be legally authorised to provide treatment that was in her best interests by the consent of someone with parental responsibility or a court order.

As this decision indicates, although a doctor can lawfully give a consenting competent child medical treatment, if the child is competent and does not consent, the doctor can still treat the child if there is consent from someone with parental responsibility for the child or an order from the court.

! Don't be tempted to . . .

'The retreat from *Gillick*'

In *Gillick,* the House of Lords made it clear that a competent child can give legally effective consent to treatment, even if a parent opposes the treatment. However, after a series of cases in the Court of Appeal following *Gillick* (e.g. *Re R (A Minor) (Wardship: Medical Treatment)* (1992)) it is clear that if the competent child does not consent to treatment, the doctor can still give the treatment if someone with parental responsibility consents. In other words, the child has the right to say 'yes', but not the right to say 'no'. Or, from the parents' perspective, they have no legal power to stop their child from receiving treatment, but they do have the legal power to authorise their child to receive treatment. It is important that you understand these distinctions. Do you think they are defensible?

The following table gives some guidance as to what factors the courts take into account in deciding whether a child is '*Gillick* competent'.

Case	Factor to be used in deciding whether child is '*Gillick* competent'
Gillick (1986)	The child must understand the medical, moral and family issues involved in the treatment
Re L (Medical Treatment: Gillick Competence) (1998)	The child had been raised as a Jehovah's Witness by her parents. The court found her incompetent in part because her 'sheltered upbringing' meant that she had limited experience of the world
Re R (A Minor) (Wardship: Consent to Medical Treatment) (1992)	A child who was fluctuating between competence and incompetence would not be regarded as *Gillick* competent
Re E (A Minor) (Wardship: Medical Treatment) (1993)	The boy did not appreciate how distressed his parents would be at his death and so his refusal to receive life-saving treatment was incompetent

Although most of the cases concerning the ability of competent children to make decisions for themselves have involved medical cases, it is clear that the approach taken there can be extended elsewhere. See, for example, *Re Roddy (A Child) (Identification: Restriction on Publication)* (2004) where a competent child was held to have the right to sell her story to the newspapers.

✎ EXAM TIP

Whenever you are discussing children's rights, always consider how the right in question is enforced and by whom. Beware of claims of children's rights that are only enforced when an adult wants that right to be enforced. For example, some claim that children have a right to have contact with their fathers, but this right seems only to be enforced when the father wants to see the child. Might this mean in reality that it is a right of the father? Or does this mean that if we take children's rights seriously, we should force unwilling fathers to have contact with their children?

■ Children in court

If children are to have rights, these must be effectively enforced. Indeed, one of the criticisms of children's rights is that they can be picked up by adults and used to pursue an adult agenda. If children's rights are to have substance, children must be able to enforce their rights and have their views heard in court.

Children can have their views heard in court in the following ways:

- Children can apply for a section 8 order. For example, in *Re SC (Leave to Seek a Residence Order)* (1994) a child sought leave to move in with her friend's family as she had fallen out with her parents. The courts rarely grant leave for such applications. They must be persuaded that the child is sufficiently competent to instruct his or her own solicitor and follow the court hearing. Leave will only be granted where the issue is not trivial and is of sufficient significance that it should be heard by the court.

- A court can direct that a report be produced by a court welfare officer, which will set out the views of the children and can affect an assessment of what order would best promote a child's welfare (*Re M (Children)* (2007)).

- A child can be joined as a party to proceedings. Normally, where a child is represented in proceedings, a **guardian ad litem** takes the role. The guardian has the job of presenting to the court a view as to what is in the child's best interests. The guardian must report the child's views to the court but is not required to recommend that the court follows them. The child can apply to have the guardian removed so that she can instruct her own solicitor to represent her views.

KEY DEFINITION: Guardian *ad litem*

A court may appoint a guardian *ad litem* (often known just as a guardian) to represent the child's interests in court. The guardian should talk to the child and inform the court of the child's views. However, the guardian is to represent the child's interests, so a guardian may inform the court that the child wants one thing but that it would be in the child's best interests for something else to happen instead.

As this shows, the courts have been rather reluctant to allow children direct access to court. The following decision might indicate that there is to be a change in attitudes.

KEY CASE

Mabon v *Mabon and Others* [2005] 2 FLR 1011 (CA)
Concerning: the representation of children in court cases

Facts

Three teenaged boys aged 13, 15 and 17 were the subject of a residence dispute between their parents. The boys wished to be separately represented, even though a guardian was representing their interests. The judge refused to allow the children to be represented and the boys appealed.

Legal principle

Thorpe LJ emphasised that in the case of mature, articulate teenagers the courts must accept they had a right to be involved in cases concerning them as part of their right to freedom of expression and respect for their family life. There was a growing acknowledgement in the law and society of children's rights to autonomy. The model of a guardian who represented the children's interests, but not necessarily their wishes, was a paternalistic model. Here the children required separate representation.

■ The Children's Commissioner

The Welsh Children's Commissioner was created by the Children's Commissioner for Wales Act 2001. The English Children's Commissioner was created by the Children Act 2004. There is an interesting contrast in their principal aims. The Welsh Commissioner's principal aim is to safeguard and promote the rights and welfare of children. The English Commissioner is to promote awareness of the views and interests of children in England. The absence of reference to rights in the English Commissioner's remit is notable. It remains to be seen how effective these commissioners will be and whether they will be able to ensure that the interests and rights of children are promoted.

✎ **EXAM TIP**

Why not visit the websites of the two commissioners so that you can tell the examiner about some of their most recent projects? The Welsh Commissioner is at **www.childcom.org.uk**. The English Commissioner is at **www.childrenscommissioner.gov.uk/**.

■ Putting it all together

Answer guidelines

See the essay question at the start of the chapter.

Approaching the question

The first part of the question asks whether the law recognises whether children have rights. It is crucial early on to define the notion of children's rights. Notice that there is disagreement among those who support children's rights over whether and when to attach more weight to children's autonomy than children's protection. So do not assume that there is a single position that is taken by all children's rights advocates. You will also need to compare a rights-based approach and a paternalistic approach, based on promoting children's welfare.

Important points to include

What you might want to do early in the essay is to highlight the differences you would expect between a legal system that was centred on children's rights and one based on children's welfare. These might include: the extent to which children can bring applications to court themselves; whether children are allowed to act on decisions they have made for themselves, even if others would consider them harmful to the child; and the extent to which children are listened to in court proceedings about themselves. You could then examine the law in these areas and see whether the law is more paternalistic or rights-based. You will want to stress that the welfare principle in the Children Act 1989 emphasises welfare, whereas the Human Rights Act 1998 provides a vehicle for the courts to enforce the rights of children. The *Gillick* decision and cases flowing from that provide a useful line of cases on which to base a discussion of whether the law places more weight on rights of autonomy or welfare.

✓ **Make your answer stand out**

On the question of whether children should have rights, there is much theoretical material, see e.g. Eekelaar (1994) and Fortin (2006). Herring (2013: chapter 8) has a useful list of the arguments against children having rights. Remember, as we have already said, that under the heading of 'rights-based approaches' a variety of different perspectives can be adopted.

READ TO IMPRESS

Bainham, A. (2009) Is Anything Now Left of Parental Rights?, in R. Probert, S. Gilmore and J. Herring (eds) *Responsible Parents and Parental Responsibility*. Oxford: Hart.

Choudhry, S. and Fenwick, H. (2005) Taking the Rights of Parents and Children Seriously: Confronting the Welfare Principle under the Human Rights Act, 25 *Oxford Journal of Legal Studies* 453.

Eekelaar, J. (1994) The Interests of the Child and the Child's Wishes: the Role of Dynamic Self-Determinism, *International Journal of Law and the Family* 42.

Fortin, J. (2006) Accommodating Children's Rights in a Post Human Rights Act Era, 69 *Modern Law Review* 299.

Gilmore, S. (2009) The Limits of Parental Responsibility, in R. Probert, S. Gilmore and J. Herring (eds) *Responsible Parents and Parental Responsibility*. Oxford: Hart.

Gilmore, S. and Herring, J. (2011) No is the Hardest Word: Consent and Children's Autonomy, *Child and Family Law Quarterly* 3.

Harris-Short, S. (2005) Family Law and the Human Rights Act 1998: Judicial Restraint or Revolution?, *Child and Family Law Quarterly* 329.

Herring, J. (1999) The Human Rights Act and the Welfare Principle in Family Law – Conflicting or Complementary?, *Child and Family Law Quarterly* 223.

Herring, J. (2005) Farewell Welfare, 27 *Journal of Social Welfare and Family Law* 159.

Herring, J. (2012) Vulnerability, Children and the Law, in M Freeman (ed), *Law and Childhood Studies*. Oxford: OUP.

Herring, J. (2013) *Family Law*. Harlow: Pearson.

Lim, H. and Roche, J. (2000) Feminism and Children's Rights, in Bridgeman, J. and Monk, D. (eds) *Feminist Perspectives on Child Law*. London: Cavendish.

Williams, J. (2005) Effective Government Structures for Children? The UK's Four Children's Commissioners, *Child and Family Law Quarterly* 37.

www.pearsoned.co.uk/lawexpress

Go online to access more revision support including quizzes to test your knowledge, sample questions with answer guidelines, podcasts you can download, and more!

Child protection

9

Revision checklist

Essential points you should know:

- [ ] The grounds for making a care order, supervision order, child assessment order and emergency protection order
- [ ] The effect of making a care order, supervision order or emergency protection order
- [ ] The duty of the local authority to protect children in need and provide accommodation

■ Topic map

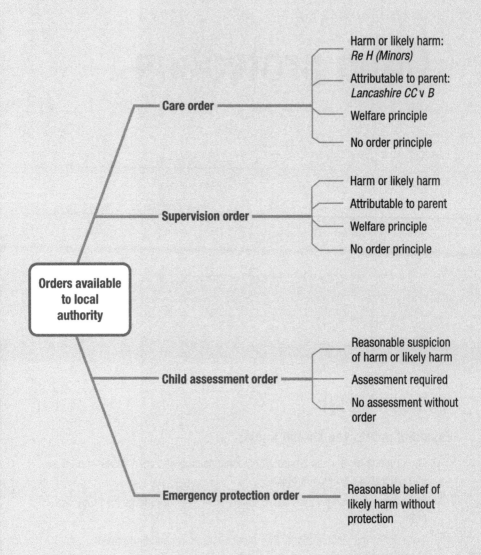

Orders available to local authority

- **Care order**
  - Harm or likely harm: *Re H (Minors)*
  - Attributable to parent: *Lancashire CC v B*
  - Welfare principle
  - No order principle

- **Supervision order**
  - Harm or likely harm
  - Attributable to parent
  - Welfare principle
  - No order principle

- **Child assessment order**
  - Reasonable suspicion of harm or likely harm
  - Assessment required
  - No assessment without order

- **Emergency protection order**
  - Reasonable belief of likely harm without protection

A printable version of this topic map is available from **www.pearsoned.co.uk/lawexpress**

■ Introduction

It seems the law on child protection always gets it wrong.

The media howl when a child is left by social workers to suffer terrible abuse at the hands of his or her parents. But they howl just as loudly when social workers remove children from 'innocent parents for no good reason'. The problem for the social worker is that the right thing to do is only obvious in retrospect. For the law, the difficulty is in setting out the circumstances in which a child can be taken into care. Set the barrier too high and children will be left unprotected. Set it too low and children will be removed from their parents without sufficient justification.

ASSESSMENT ADVICE

Essay questions

Essays on child protection often centre around the interpretation of the threshold criteria in section 31, Children Act 1989, which set out the circumstances in which a care or supervision order is made. The cases interpreting these can be seen as requiring a delicate balance between protecting the interests of the parents in having their children removed improperly and protecting children from abuse by ensuring that if they are in danger they can be protected. This is an area where the Human Rights Act has played a significant role and so it is useful to bring into an essay a discussion of how a human rights approach could be applied in this area.

Problem questions

Problem questions tend to ask you to consider what orders could be sought by a local authority in a troublesome scenario. Remember to discuss the range of options. There is quite a bit of case law now interpreting the threshold criteria and it draws some fine distinctions, which you will need to be able to explain clearly to produce a good answer. You should also refer to Human Rights Act arguments as this is an area where the courts appear particularly amenable to such arguments (see e.g. *Re S (Minors)* (2010)).

■ Sample question

Could you answer this question? Below is a typical problem question that could arise on this topic. Guidelines on answering the question are included at the end of this chapter; a sample essay question and guidance on tackling it can be found on the companion website.

PROBLEM QUESTION

Evander, aged 10, lives with his mother, Luscinda, a lone parent. Luscinda is devoutly religious and requires Evander to spend two hours a day locked in his room in prayer. He is also not allowed to talk to any girls. Social workers were alerted by Evander's school because he appeared unhappy and withdrawn. Social workers were also contacted by Evander's doctor, because at a recent examination of Evander, she spotted some bruises that could indicate sexual abuse. When asked about these, Luscinda said that they were nothing to do with her, but that Evander did spend one day a week with his Uncle Obadiah and the marks could have been caused by him. Further medical examination is unable to establish whether or not there is sexual abuse, but an expert states that there is a 40% chance that there is. There is no medical evidence to establish who it might be who is sexually abusing Evander, if anyone.

Advise the local authority on what steps it could take to protect Evander and the likely success of any application the local authority might make.

■ The protection of children from abuse

Article 19(1) of the United Nations Convention on the Rights of the Child states that states should take all appropriate legislative, administrative, social and educational measures to protect the child from violence and abuse. The duty on the state to protect children from abuse can also be found in the European Convention on Human Rights. The law, however, has a delicate balance to strike: protecting children from abuse at the hands of their families, while not subjecting the children to abuse by removing them from families wrongly suspected to be abusers.

The Children Act 1989, in Part III, seeks to ensure that children do not reach the position in which they have to be taken into care. For example, local authorities have a duty to provide services to children in need in their area, under section 17. They also have a duty to accommodate children in section 20 if there is a need for that.

■ The threshold criteria

The start for lawyers considering a child protection case is to consider whether the 'threshold criteria' are met. For the exam you will need to have a good understanding of the criteria and the case law explaining them. These criteria, set out in section 31(2), must be met if the court is to make a care order or supervision order. If they are not met, the court will be restricted to considering some of the less interventionist orders. If they are met the court can make a care order if doing so will promote the welfare of the child.

KEY STATUTE

Children Act 1989, section 31(2)

'A court may only make a care order or supervision order if it is satisfied –

(a) that the child concerned is suffering, or is likely to suffer, significant harm; and

(b) that the harm, or likelihood of harm, is attributable to –

    (i) the care given to the child, or likely to be given to him if the order were not made, not being what it would be reasonable to expect a parent to give to him;

    (ii) the child's being beyond parental control.'

The interpretation of these threshold criteria is not straightforward. The following issues of interpretation are ones that are particularly likely to come up in the exam:

- Harm means ill-treatment or the impairment of health or development. It can include impairment caused by witnessing someone suffering ill-treatment, e.g. domestic violence. To amount to significant harm it must be enough to justify the intervention of the state into family life (*Re MA (Care Threshold)* (2009)). There had to be something more than commonplace human failure or inadequacy, but the conduct does not have to be intentional or deliberate (*Re B (A Child)* (2013)).

- Development here includes physical, intellectual, emotional, social or behavioural development. Health includes physical or mental health. Ill-treatment includes sexual abuse.

- To decide if the child is suffering harm, a comparison must be made with what could be expected of a similar child of the same intellectual and social development: *Re O (A Minor) (Care Proceedings: Education)* (1992).

- The law must tolerate diverse standards of parenting and understand that not every parent can be expected to be perfect: *Re L (A Child) (Care: Threshold Criteria)* (2007).

- Where it is claimed that the child is likely to suffer harm, the court will consider whether the child was likely to suffer harm at the time when the local authority first intervened to protect the family. So, if the local authority has removed the child from a violent family and the child at the time of application is with a loving foster carer, it cannot be argued that the child is not currently suffering harm and so the threshold criteria are not met: *Re M (A Minor) (Care Order: Threshold Criteria)* (1994).

- To be 'likely' to suffer significant harm, there had to be a 'real possibility' that harm would be suffered (*Re B (A Child)* (2013)).

- The question of what the burden of proof is in the application is settled by *Re H (Minors) (Sexual Abuse: Standard of Proof)* (1996), see below.

- A care order could be made if it was unclear the significant harm was caused either by a parent or someone else involved in the care of a child (*Lancashire CC* v *B* (2000)). However, the threshold criteria would not be made out if it was unclear whether the harm was caused by a parent or a stranger.

KEY CASE

Re H (Minors) (Sexual Abuse: Standard of Proof) [1996] AC 563 (HL)
Concerning: the threshold criteria in section 31, Children Act 1989

Facts

A local authority applied for a care order in respect of girls aged 13, 8 and 2. Their older sister had claimed that she had been sexually abused by their mother's cohabitant. He had been charged with rape but had been acquitted. The applications for a care order were dismissed.

Legal principle

(i) The standard of proof in care proceedings was the balance of probabilities. It needed to be shown that it was more likely than not that the children had suffered or were likely to suffer significant harm. However, where there was an allegation of particularly serious harm, more evidence would be required to show that it had probably occurred than would be the case of an allegation of less serious harm.

(ii) Where it was claimed that it was likely that the children were to suffer significant harm, 'likely' meant that there was a real possibility that they would. It did not need to be shown that it was more likely than not that the children would suffer significant harm.

(iii) If it is claimed that the children are likely to suffer harm, this must be shown on the basis of facts, rather than suspicions. So the local authority will need to establish on the balance of probabilities that certain facts occurred, and then argue that from them it can be said that there is a real risk that the children will suffer significant harm.

Applying these to the case at hand, because it had not been proved on the balance of probabilities that the father had abused the older girl, there were no facts on which to establish that there was a risk to the younger ones.

! Don't be tempted to . . .

Burdens of proof

The speech of Lord Nicholls in *Re H* causes students many problems, especially his statements about the burden of proof. It is a relief that we now have the decision in *Re B*, which clarifies the law. The position is this: the burden of proof is on the balance of probabilities (confirmed again in *Re S-B (Children)* (2009)). In other words, it must be shown as more likely than not that the child has suffered or is likely to suffer harm. However, Lord Nicholls stated that the more serious the allegation, the more evidence would be needed to show that it had happened or was likely to happen. His point is that some things are inherently less likely to be true. If I were to tell you that I had seen the Queen yesterday and showed you a photograph of me standing in a crowd near the Queen, you would probably be persuaded that I was telling the truth. If, however, I were to tell you that I had seen a green man from Mars and showed you a photograph of me by an alien, you would probably still not be convinced. You would, in fact, need a lot of evidence to be persuaded of that. In *Re B* Baroness Hale explained that it was fair to say that facts that were inherently unlikely were harder to prove on the balance of probabilities. Where Lord Nicholls had gone wrong was to suggest serious allegations were inherently unlikely. So, the current position is that when considering whether or not the allegation has been proved, the fact that it is inherently unlikely is a factor to take into account, but not the severity of the allegation. Sometimes the courts cannot determine who was the perpetrator of the harm, in which case they should try and produce a list of possible perpetrators (*Re S-B* (2009)).

KEY CASE

Re J (Children) [2013] UKSC 9
Concerning: proving the threshold criteria

Facts

The mother and her partner lived with three children. The mother's first child (TL) had died in 2004 from non-accidental injuries. Care proceedings had been brought then and the judge concluded that either the mother or her ex-partner had caused the injuries. They were both 'possible perpetrators'. Care proceedings were brought in relation to the three children now living with the mother on the basis that because she was a 'possible perpetrator' of abuse to a child in the past, there was a real possibility that the children now living with her were likely to suffer significant harm.

Legal principle

The Supreme Court held that courts could only find the threshold criteria established based on facts proved on the balance of probability. Suspicions could not be used. In this case it had not been established that the mother had harmed her first child and so there were no proven facts that could be used to establish the risk of significant harm.

> **!** **Don't be tempted to . . .**
>
> Don't assume that if the threshold criteria are met the court must make a care order. The threshold criteria permit, but do not require, the court to make a care or supervision order. In *Re B (Children)* (2012) even though the children were at risk of suffering significant harm the court determined it was better not to make a care order but instead help the parents be better parents.

■ The making of a care order

The definition of a care order

KEY STATUTE

Children Act 1989, section 33(1) and (3)

1 Where a care order is made with respect to a child it shall be the duty of the local authority designated by the order to receive the child into their care and to keep him in their care while the order remains in force.

[. . .]

3 While a care order is in force in respect to a child, the local authority designated by the order shall –

Step 1. (a) have parental responsibility for the child; and

Step 2. (b) have the power (subject to the following provisions of this section) to determine the extent to which –

    (i) a parent, guardian or special guardian of the child; or

    (ii) a person who by virtue of section 4A has parental responsibility for the child, may meet his parental responsibility for him.'

A care order, then, authorises the local authority to remove children from their parents. But notice that it does not require a local authority to do that. It is perfectly possible, and quite common, for a local authority to have a care order for a child, but to leave the child with her/his parents. Note, however, that in such a case the local authority can remove the child without needing to make any further application to the court. The local authority will have parental responsibility for the child and can decide the extent to which the parents are allowed to care for the child. However, section 34 of the Children Act 1989 creates a presumption in favour of allowing a child in care to have contact with his or her parents. Section 34(2) does permit a local authority to apply for a court order that contact cease.

The grounds for making a care order

In order to make a care order, the court must be persuaded that the threshold criteria are made out; that the making of a care order will promote the child's welfare; and that making a care order will be better for the child than making no order at all.

✎ EXAM TIP

Do not make the error of assuming that because the threshold criteria in section 31(2) are made out that the court is entitled to make a care order or supervision order. The court must also be persuaded that the order is in the best interests of the child. It is perfectly open for the court to decide that the threshold criteria are met, but that it will be in the welfare of the child not to make an order.

When deciding whether making the care order will promote the welfare of the child, the courts will consider the notion of **proportionality**. This is a central doctrine under the jurisprudence of the European Court of Human Rights.

KEY DEFINITION: Proportionality

Proportionality has become a key concept in child protection law, especially since the advent of the Human Rights Act 1998. It requires the degree of intervention into family life to be proportionate to the risk faced by the child. Further, it requires the courts to authorise an intervention to protect a child only if it is the least intrusive measure into family life that will adequately protect the child. So, if a supervision order will adequately protect the child, the court should not make the more intrusive care order.

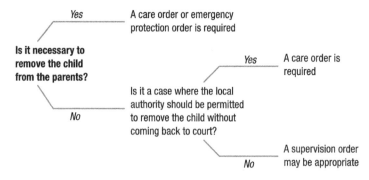

The effect of a care order

Once a care order has been made, it is for the local authority to decide how to use its parental responsibility. The court cannot attach conditions to a care order. A local authority is required to prepare a **care plan**, setting out what it intends to do with the child after the care order is made. However, it is free to depart from the care plan once the order is made, without having to seek permission of the courts. That was made clear in the following case: *Re S, Re W (Children: Care Plan)* (2002).

KEY CASE

Re S, Re W (Children: Care Plan) [2002] 1 FCR 577 (HL)

Concerning: the enforceability of care plans

Facts

Two cases were brought before the Court of Appeal seeking guidance on the extent to which a court when making a care order could require the local authority to abide by the care plan produced by the local authority in support of its application. The Court of Appeal held that when making a care order, the court could star items on the care plan. If a local authority subsequently wished to depart from the starred proposals, court permission would be required. The local authority appealed to the House of Lords.

Legal principle

The House of Lords held that the approach of the Court of Appeal was illegitimate. There was nothing in the Children Act that authorised the Court of Appeal's order and the Human Rights Act could not be used to read words into legislation. The Children Act had created a fundamental distinction between the role of the courts, which was to decide whether or not to make a care order, and the role of the local authority, which was to decide how to implement the care plan. The Court of Appeal had wrongly tried to compel the local authority to treat a child in care in a particular way.

■ The supervision order

The definition of a supervision order

KEY STATUTE

Children Act 1989, 35(1)

'While a supervision order is in force it shall be the duty of the supervisor –

(a) to advise, assist and befriend the supervised child;
(b) to take such steps as are reasonably necessary to give effect to the order; and
(c) where –
  (i) the order is not wholly complied with; or
  (ii) the supervisor considers that the order may no longer be necessary to consider whether or not to apply to the court for its variation or discharge.'

The supervision order imposes a duty on the supervisor to advise, befriend and assist the child. The obligations it imposes upon the parents are very limited. However, always lurking behind the supervision order is the threat that if the parents do not cooperate with the supervisor, a care order may be sought.

The grounds for making a supervision order

The supervision order can only be made where the court is satisfied that the threshold criteria are made out, and that making a supervision order will promote the welfare of the child, and that making an order is better than making no order at all.

■ Emergencies

In a problem question you will need to decide whether the situation requires immediate intervention. Where there is an emergency, an application can be made under section 44 for an emergency protection order. However, in *Re X (Emergency Protection Orders)* (2006), Munby J said they should be used sparingly and only as a last resort. The grounds for applying for an order is reasonable cause to suspect that the threshold criteria are made out; or that the local authority is trying to make enquiries about a child and is unreasonably being frustrated access to the child. The order permits a local authority to remove children from their parents. The order can be made without giving the parents notice of the application, but it cannot last more than eight days, although it can be extended for a further seven. When the order comes to an end, the child must be returned to the parents, or an application for a care order must be made.

As well as the emergency protection order, the police have the power to remove a child to suitable accommodation if they have reasonable cause to believe that otherwise the child would be likely to suffer significant harm. The power only lasts for 72 hours.

■ Alternative orders

If a care order or supervision order is not appropriate, there are other possibilities for a local authority. Of course, where the parents are happy to receive the help of the local authority, it is probably unnecessary to seek any order at all. Under section 20 of the Children Act 1989 if a child is in need and requires accommodation, that can be provided by the local authority if the parent consents.

The local authority could apply for a Child Assessment order under section 43. This is an order enabling medical or psychiatric assessment of the child to take place. In broad terms, it is necessary to show that there are reasonable grounds to suspect that the child is suffering or is likely to suffer significant harm and that the assessment will help establish whether or not this is the case.

Under section 17 the local authority is under a duty to safeguard and promote the welfare of children in their area who are in need. It should provide a range of services appropriate to the needs. Note that this duty cannot be enforced by an individual seeking to be provided services (*R (G)* v *Barnet LBC* (2004)).

■ Putting it all together

Answer guidelines

See the problem question at the start of the chapter.

Approaching the question

The starting point in a problem like this is to ascertain whether or not the threshold criteria in section 31 of the Children Act 1989 have been made out.

Important points to include

There are a number of issues here.

- Can the hours of prayer constitute harm? Is Evander to be compared to a child of his cultural background or an average child?
- If the local authority relies on the feared abuse, has it been shown on the balance of probabilities that there is a real risk of harm? Notice here that although it is not more likely than not that there has been abuse (it has been put at a 40% chance), it has been shown (if the report is by a reputable expert relying on a medical examination) as more likely than not that there is a real risk of harm in the future. That is sufficient to meet the threshold criteria.
- Discuss the issue of whether it matters that it is unclear whether Luscinda or Obadiah is responsible (see *Lancashire CC* v *B*).

You will also want to consider the different orders that the local authority could apply for.

✓ **Make your answer stand out**

Remembering that the proportionality principle requires the court to make the least intrusive order that will adequately protect Evander, consider the human rights issues raised by the case.

READ TO IMPRESS

Bailey-Harris, R. and Harris, M. (2002) Local Authorities and Child Protection – the Mosaic of Accountability, *Child and Family Law Quarterly* 117.

Cobley, C. and Lowe, N. (2009) Interpreting the Threshold Criteria under Section 31(2) of the Children Act 1989, *Modern Law Review* 463.

Cobley, C. and Lowe, N. (2011) The Statutory "Threshold" under Section 31 of the Children Act 1989 – Time to Take Stock, *Law Quarterly Review* 396.

Hayes, M. (1998) Child Protection – from Principles and Policies to Practice, *Child and Family Law Quarterly* 119.

Hayes, M. (2004) Uncertain Evidence and Risk Taking in Child Protection Cases, *Child and Family Law Quarterly* 63.

Kaganas, F. (2010) Child Protection, Gender and Rights, in Wallbank, J., Choudhry, S. and Herring, J. (eds) *Rights, Gender and Family Law*. Abingdon: Routledge.

Masson, J. (2000) From Curtis to Waterhouse, in Katz, S., Eekelaar, J. and MacLean, M. (eds) *Cross Currents*. Oxford: OUP.

Masson, J. (2005) Emergency Intervention to Protect Children: Using and Avoiding Legal Controls, *Child and Family Law Quarterly* 75.

Murphy, J. (2003) Children in Need: the Limits of Local Authority Accountability, *Legal Studies* 104.

www.pearsoned.co.uk/lawexpress

Go online to access more revision support including quizzes to test your knowledge, sample questions with answer guidelines, podcasts you can download, and more!

Adoption

10

Revision checklist

Essential points you should know:

- [ ] Who can adopt children and which children can be adopted
- [ ] The grounds for making an adoption order or special guardianship
- [ ] The law surrounding 'open adoption'
- [ ] How adopted children can discover who their birth parents were

■ Topic map

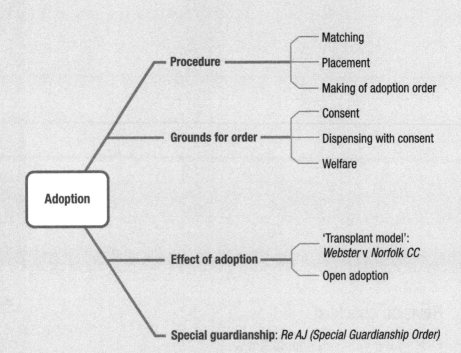

- **Procedure**
  - Matching
  - Placement
  - Making of adoption order
- **Grounds for order**
  - Consent
  - Dispensing with consent
  - Welfare
- **Adoption**
- **Effect of adoption**
  - 'Transplant model': *Webster* v *Norfolk CC*
  - Open adoption
- **Special guardianship**: *Re AJ (Special Guardianship Order)*

A printable version of this topic map is available from **www.pearsoned.co.uk/lawexpress**

■ Introduction

The government is convinced we need to increase the number of children being adopted.

It argues that the security and formality offered by adoption provides the best setting for children who can no longer live with their parents. However, others are not convinced. Adoption means the severing of formal legal ties with the birth parents and wider family. It means all hope of reuniting the parents and children has been lost. There are a number of key legal issues here. The first are the grounds that need to be established before an adoption order can be made. The second is the effect of the adoption order and, in particular, what links, if any, the child has with the birth family. The third is the ability of the adopted child to find out information about his or her birth family.

ASSESSMENT ADVICE

Essay questions

The law on adoption has been radically changed with the Adoption and Children Act of 2002. As yet, there is very little case law on it. However, you can use cases decided under the old law to demonstrate some of the issues that may well arise under the new legislation. You should always be familiar with the key provisions in the legislation and particularly the circumstances in which the consent of the parents to placement or adoption can be dispensed with. The Human Rights Act may have a role to play here, although it remains to be seen how receptive the courts will be to arguments based on that legislation. Don't forget the option of special guardianship as an alternative to adoption. Essay questions are likely to focus either on the protection of the interests of the birth family in adoption cases or on the role that adoption plays generally in the law in this area.

Problem questions

Problem questions are likely to focus on the grounds for making the adoption; the issue of 'open adoption' and the status of the child while being placed prior to the making of the adoption. You will need to be familiar with the key legislative provisions and be able to make arguments over the ambiguities in the law. It is particularly important that you are familiar with the law on dispensing with consent to adoption as this nearly always appears on a problem question on adoption.

Sample question

Could you answer this essay question? Below is a typical essay question that could arise on this topic. Guidelines on answering the question are included at the end of this chapter; a sample problem question and guidance on tackling it can be found on the companion website.

ESSAY QUESTION

Does the Adoption and Children Act 2002 adequately protect the interests of the birth family?

Who can be adopted?

It is easy to make some foolish comments when writing about adoption based on a misperception of adoption in reality. There are two points to emphasise. First, it is very rare for babies to be adopted. It is far more common for children to have spent some time with their parents before being removed by the local authority. The significance of this is that many children will know their parents and so the kind of secrecy that used to pervade adoption (when children were not told they were adopted) is almost unheard of nowadays. The second point is that adoption is rare. In 2013 there were about 68,000 children in care, with only about 4,000 children being placed for adoption.

! Don't be tempted to . . .

Adoption in practice
It is only possible to make an adoption order in respect of a child who is under 18 at the time of the adoption proceedings. You can adopt your own child. This might be appropriate where you get rid of the status of the other parent. As you can imagine, the courts will require some convincing of this. More common is where a parent and step-parent adopt so that the step-parent can become legally the parent of the child.

◼ Who can adopt?

The 2002 Adoption and Children Act greatly increased the range of people who can apply. They now include:

- ◼ married couples;
- ◼ civil partners;
- ◼ a cohabiting couple (whether same-sex or opposite-sex);
- ◼ a single person.

However, an applicant must be over 21.

◼ The adoption procedure

The law governing the procedure of adoption is complex. In outline, it involves the following steps.

Stage in the procedure	Purpose
Local authority decides that adoption is appropriate for this child	An assessment that there is no realistic hope of successfully returning the child to his or her parents
Assessing adopters	The adoption agency ensures that the applicant or applicants are suitable to adopt children
Matching the adopters and child	The agency decides which applicants are suitable for which children available for adoption
Placement of the child with the adopters	The child lives with the adopters as a kind of trial run to see if the adoption might work
The agency applies for an adoption order that the court may make	The court must be persuaded that there is the necessary appropriate parental consent (or that requirement has been dispensed with) and that the adoption is in the child's best interests

The most controversial aspects of the procedure are the placing of the child with the adopters and the making of the adoption order, so we shall focus on those.

▓ Placement of the child

KEY DEFINITION: Placement

This is where the child lives with the would-be adopters as a form of 'trial' period to see if the adoption is likely to work. Note that a child can only be placed if the 'placement conditions' are met, which most importantly require the parents to have consented to the making of the adoption order or for their consent to have been dispensed with.

An adoption agency can place a child with adopters either with the consent of the birth parents (under section 19) or by means of a **placement** order (under section 21). Before making a placement order, the court must be satisfied that:

- ▪ the child is in care or the threshold conditions under Children Act 1989, section 31(2) have been made out or the child has no parent or guardian;
- ▪ the making of the placement order is in the welfare of the child;
- ▪ the parents of the child have consented or the consent of the parents has been dispensed with.

Of this list, you need to know more about two factors: the welfare test and the dispensing with consent test.

The welfare of the child in adoption cases

When deciding what is in the welfare of the child, the following provisions apply.

KEY STATUTE

Adoption and Children Act 2002, section 1(2)

The 'paramount consideration of the court or adoption agency must be the child's welfare throughout his life'.

KEY STATUTE

Adoption and Children Act 2002, section 1(4)

Here is the list of factors that the court should take into account in any decisions relating to welfare in the adoption context:

(a) the child's ascertainable wishes and feelings regarding the decision (considered in the light of the child's age and understanding);

(b) the child's particular needs;

(c) the likely effect on the child (throughout his or her life) of having ceased to be a member of the original family and become an adopted person;

(d) the child's age, sex, background and any of the child's characteristics which the court or agency considers relevant;

(e) any harm (within the meaning of the Children Act 1989) which the child has suffered or is at risk of suffering;

(f) the relationship the child has with relatives and with any other person in relation to whom the court or agency considers the relationship to be relevant, including –

(i) the likelihood of any such relationship continuing and the value to the child of its doing so;

(ii) the ability and willingness of any of the child's relatives, or of any such person, to provide the child with a secure environment in which to develop, and otherwise to meet the child's needs;

(iii) the wishes and feelings of any of the child's relatives, or of any such person, regarding the child.'

✎ EXAM TIP

When considering the welfare principle in the Adoption and Children Act 2002 (ACA), it is worth noticing that the welfare test in section 1 of the Act is slightly different from the welfare principle in the Children Act 1989. First, notice that the ACA specifically tells the court to consider the position of the child into adulthood. Second, the factors in section 1(4), ACA are like those in section 1(3), CA 1989, but not identical. In particular, note section 1(4)(f), ACA and the reference to the child's wider relationships, and in section 1(4)(c) the significance of ceasing to be a member of the wider birth family.

Particularly relevant in deciding whether there should be a placement order is factor (f): the relationship the child has with any relatives. In practice, if a child cannot be cared for by his or her parents, the courts will consider whether or not the child should be looked after by the child's wider family. Only if that is not possible will adoption outside the family be considered.

Dispensing with consent

In order to make a placement order, it is necessary to have parental consent. But who exactly must consent? All parents or guardians or **special guardians** with parental responsibility must consent. However, the consent of an unmarried father without parental responsibility is not required. That said, an unmarried father will normally be informed of the proceedings and given a chance to have his say. Indeed, a failure to do so could amount to a breach of his rights under the Human Rights Act 1998.

If all those with parental responsibility have consented, there is no problem. But if one of the required consents is not forthcoming, a court will have to dispense with the consent. The test for doing that is set out in section 52(1), Adoption and Children Act 2002.

KEY STATUTE

Adoption and Children Act 2002, section 52(1)

'The court cannot dispense with the consent of any parent or guardian of a child to the child being placed for adoption or to the making of an adoption order in respect of the child unless the court is satisfied that –

(a) the parent or guardian cannot be found or is incapable of giving consent, or

(b) the welfare of the child requires the consent to be dispensed with.'

In deciding whether the welfare of the child requires the consent to be dispensed with, the court will take into account the checklist of factors in section 1(4), Adoption and Children Act 2002 (listed earlier). In *Re Q (A Child)* (2011) the Court of Appeal stated that the word 'requires' indicated that the child's welfare made adoption necessary.

! Don't be tempted to . . .

Dispensing with consent
Section 52 at first reading appears to permit the court to dispense with the consent of the parent if that would be in the welfare of the child. Indeed, it has been criticised for allowing the courts to dispense with consent too easily. However, notice that the provision is not as wide as might at first appear. First, it must be shown that the child's welfare *requires* the parent's consent to be dispensed with. It might be argued that if the adoption is very slightly in the welfare of the child, that is insufficient to mean that the adoption is required. Second, the legislation must be read in a way that is in compliance with the European Convention on Human Rights, in so far as that is possible. The European Court of Human Rights has indicated that adoption should only be used if there is no realistic prospect of the child being reunited with the parents.

■ The effect of an adoption order

Under Adoption and Children Act 2002, section 67(1) 'an adopted person is to be treated in law as the child of the adopters or adopter'. This reflects the 'transplant model' of adoption. The child will cease to be the child of the birth parents for legal purposes and will become the child of the adopters. Once an adoption order has been made, it will only be revoked in exceptional circumstances (*Webster* v *Norfolk CC* [2009] EWCA 59).

Sitting rather uncomfortably with the 'transplant model' is the current popularity for 'open adoption'. This is the idea that the adopted children will retain contact with their birth families. Section 46(6) of the Act requires the court before making an adoption order to consider whether there should be arrangements for contact with the child. However, that is not the same as saying the court must make such arrangements unless there is a good reason not to; it must just consider the issue. Generally, then, where contact does take place between adopted children and their birth families, this is done as a matter of 'good will' rather than the result of a formal order.

Adopted children and birth information

Many children who have been adopted wish to discover information about their birth family. Children who have attained the age of 18 can obtain a copy of their birth certificate from the Registrar-General. This will be provided unless there are good public policy reasons not to give this. Under sections 77 and 78 of the Adoption and Children Act 2002 there will also be an Adoption Children Register, giving the details of all adoptions.

Any person can receive a copy of any entry in the Register. A child under the age of 18 can even seek a copy of an entry in the Register, under certain conditions.

Special guardianship

KEY DEFINITION: Special guardian

The status of special guardian was created in the Adoption and Children Act 2002. It is designed to be more secure than merely giving someone a residence order, but does not have the effect that an adoption has of ending the relationship between the child and birth family. The special guardian has parental responsibility and can exercise that to the exclusion of the child's parents or others with parental responsibility.

The following people can apply for a special guardianship order if over 18 years old:

- a guardian of a child;
- a person with a residence order in respect of the child;
- a person who has the consent of all those with a residence order or all those with parental responsibility;
- any person with whom the child has lived for three of the five previous years, provided that they have the consent of a person with parental responsibility or the local authority (if the child is in care);
- a local authority foster-parent with whom the child has lived for a period of one year.

People not in this list need the leave of the court to apply.

When considering an application for a special guardianship order, the court will be bound to apply the welfare principle in section 1, Children Act 1989. The court may consider whether special guardianship is more or less appropriate than adoption. The following table compares and contrasts the effects of adoption and special guardianship.

Adoption	Special guardianship (SG)
Adoption brings to an end the parental status of the birth family	With SG the birth family retains its parental status
The adoptive parents acquire parental responsibility and the full status of parents	A special guardian is not the parent of the child, but has parental responsibility for the child and can exercise it to the exclusion of any other person with it
An adoption can be brought to an end only by another adoption order	SG can be brought to an end by an application to the court, although leave of the court is required before such an application can be made

In *Re AJ (A Child) (Special Guardianship Order)* (2007) the Court of Appeal rejected an argument that special guardianship rather than adoption should be used where relatives were going to care for a child. The court emphasised that in every case the court must simply decide which order will best promote the welfare of the child.

✎ EXAM TIP

In a problem question, you will need to consider whether the case is one where special guardianship or adoption is more appropriate. The main benefit of adoption is the security it offers and the sense of belonging to the adoptive family. The special guardianship means that the link with the birth family is retained. This may be seen as both its main strength and weakness.

There are other options apart from adoption and special guardianship. These include a residence order or granting step-parents parental responsibility.

■ Putting it all together

Answer guidelines

See the essay question at the start of the chapter.

Approaching the question

Start by setting out the current law, before considering whether it strikes the correct balance.

Important points to include

There are several key issues you will want to raise in discussing the question posed in this essay:

- Does the ground for dispensing with consent adequately protect the rights of the birth parents?
- Is the rule that if consent to adoption is given at the placement stage it cannot be withdrawn too harsh? Or is it necessary to protect the interests of the adopters?
- Should the law take a stricter line in encouraging open adoption?
- Is the transplant model inappropriate?
- Is it justifiable for the law to permit adoption by step-parents?

✓ Make your answer stand out

Consider whether the Human Rights Act 1998 is significant here. Consider also the weight in other areas of family law that is attached to the biological connection between a parent and child.

READ TO IMPRESS

Ball, C. (2005) The Adoption and Children Act 2002 – A Critical Examination, 29 *Adoption and Fostering* 6.

Choudhry, S. (2003) The Adoption and Children Act 2002: the Welfare Principle and the Human Rights Act 1998 – a Missed Opportunity, *Child and Family Law Quarterly* 119.

Cullen, H. (2005) Adoption – a (Fairly) New Approach, *Child and Family Law Quarterly* 475.

Harris-Short, S. (2001) The Adoption and Children Bill – a Fast Track to Failure?, *Child and Family Law Quarterly* 405.

Harris-Short, S. (2008) Making and Breaking Family Life: Adoption, the State and Human Rights, 14 *Journal of Law and Society* 325.

Sloan, B. (2009) Welfare and the Rights of the Birth Family in "Fast Track" Adoption Cases, *Child and Family Law Quarterly* 87.

www.pearsoned.co.uk/lawexpress

Go online to access more revision support including quizzes to test your knowledge, sample questions with answer guidelines, podcasts you can download, and more!

And finally, before the exam . . .

You should by now be at a reasonable stage in your revision process. If you have grasped the material in this book, you will have the basic tools you need to tackle an exam in family law. You will need to do more thinking and reading to build on what is set out here, but you are well on your way to doing well.

Never forget that family law is about real people – people with their flaws, their weaknesses, and motivated not by a desire to comply with the law but by the strongest of emotions. And never forget the weakness of family law. Law cannot make broken relationships better again; it cannot make children happy; and it cannot provide perfect justice. What it can do is to provide people with some tools that might, just might, help them to make something out of the mess they have got into.

Test yourself

☐ Look at the **revision checklists** at the start of each chapter. Are you happy that you can now tick them all? If not, go back to the particular chapter and work through the material again. If you are still struggling, seek help from your tutor.

☐ Attempt the **sample questions** in each chapter and check your answers against the guidelines provided.

☐ Go online to **www.pearsoned.co.uk/lawexpress** for more hands-on revision help and try out these resources:

☐ Try the **test your knowledge** quizzes and see if you can score full marks for each chapter.

☐ Attempt to answer the **sample questions** for each chapter within the time limit and check your answers against the guidelines provided.

☐ Listen to the **podcast** and then attempt the question it discusses. ▶

☐ **'You be the marker'** and see if you can spot the strengths and weaknesses of the sample answers.

☐ Use the **flashcards** to test your recall of the legal principles of the key cases and statutes you've revised and the definitions of important terms.

☐ Keep an eye out for family law issues in the newspapers.

■ Linking it all up

Do not regard family law as a series of discrete boxes. There are many issues that run through the different chapters. Examiners will be particularly impressed if you can show how there are similarities between the issues that arise in one topic and those in another. Check where there are overlaps between subject areas. (You may want to review the 'revision note' boxes throughout this book.) Make a careful note of these, as knowing how one topic may lead into another can increase your marks significantly. Here are some examples:

✔ The tension between seeing parenthood as based on biology or care.

✔ Whether family law should be based on fixed rules or adopt a discretionary approach so that each case can be dealt with on its own facts.

✔ What role does gender play in family law? Are there too many or too few distinctions between men and women, mothers and fathers in family law?

■ Knowing your cases

Make sure you know how to use relevant case law in your answers. Use the table below to focus your revision of the key cases in each topic. To review the details of these cases, refer back to the particular chapter.

Key case	How to use	Related topics
Chapter 1 – Marriage and civil partnership		
R (on the application of the CPS) v Registrar General	To show the law will not stop a marriage entered for bad motives	Autonomy of parties

Key case	How to use	Related topics
Sheffield City Council v *E*	To define capacity for marriage	Nature of marriage
Chapter 2 – Cohabitation		
Ghaidan v *Godin-Mendoza*	To define 'spouse'	Civil partnerships; human rights
Lloyds Bank v *Rossett*	To describe criteria for a constructive trust	Cohabitants
Jones v *Kernott*	To describe how to find parties' intention	Cohabitants
Thorner v *Major*	To explain the nature of a proprietary estoppel	Cohabitants; constructive trust
Sutton v *Mishcon de Reya*	To set out law on cohabitation contracts	Same-sex couples; autonomy
Chapter 3 – Domestic violence		
Yemshaw v *London Borough of Hounslow*	To define domestic violence	Gender; human rights
C v *C (Non-Molestation Order)*	To explain the meaning of molestation	Violence
Re Y (Children) (Occupation Order)	To describe how the court decides whether to make an occupation order	Property interests; domestic violence
Lau v *DPP*	To discuss when the court will make an order under the Protection from Harassment Act	Violence
Chapter 4 – Divorce		
Buffery v *Buffery*	To explain the ground for divorce	Nature of marriage; autonomy
Cleary v *Cleary*	To define adultery	Gender
Birch v *Birch*	To describe unreasonable behaviour	Fault

▶

Key case	How to use	Related topics
Chapter 5 – Financial issues on divorce and dissolution		
White v *White*	To establish the principle of equality	Gender; divorce
Miller v *Miller; McFarlane* v *McFarlane*	To discuss the principle of compensation	Fault
Charman v *Charman*	To discuss the nature of contributions	Gender; equality
McCartney v *Mills McCartney*	An example of application of the law	Sharing
Radmacher v *Granatino*	To discuss the enforceability of pre-nups	Nature of marriage; autonomy
Barder v *Barder*	To consider when an order may be varied	Divorce; fault
Chapter 6 – Who is a parent?		
A v *Leeds Teaching Hospital NHS Trust*	To define a father	Gender; assisted reproduction
Re S (Parental Responsibility)	To examine when a father should be given parental responsibility	Fault; gender
M v *M (Parental Responsibility)*	To give an example of when a father should not have parental responsibility	Parenthood; human rights
Chapter 7 – Resolving disputes over children's upbringing		
Re G (Children)	To discuss the significance of the natural parenthood	Gender; parental responsibility; same-sex couple
Re B (A Child) (Residence Order)	To consider the nature of the natural parent presumption	Grandparents
Re L, V, M and H	To examine when a contact order should be made	Domestic violence

Key case	How to use	Related topics
Chapter 8 – Children's rights		
Gillick v *West Norfolk and Wisbech HA*	To discuss when children can make medical decisions for themselves	Contraception; parental rights
Re R (A Minor) (Wardship: Medical Treatment)	To consider when a parent can consent on behalf of a child	Parental responsibility
Mabon v *Mabon*	To provide an example of children being represented in court	Autonomy; welfare principle
Chapter 9 – Child protection		
Re H (Minors) (Sexual Abuse: Standard of Proof)	To explain the threshold criteria	Harm; sexual abuse
Re J (Children)	To discuss how the threshold criteria can be proved	Parental rights
Re S; *Re W*	To give an example of the legal effect of care plans	Welfare principle; human rights

■ Sample question

Below is an essay question that incorporates overlapping areas of the law. See if you can answer it drawing upon your knowledge of the whole subject area. Guidelines on answering this question are included at the end of this section.

ESSAY QUESTION

What role, if any, does fault play in family law?

■ Putting it all together

Answer guidelines

Approaching the question

You could explain that family law originated in the church courts. It is not surprising that fault and moral blame played such a big role. You can then consider the role it plays in the law now.

Important points to make

Fault used to be an extremely important factor in family law cases. A person could only get divorced if they could show that their spouse had behaved in a particularly bad way. If a person was seen to have behaved immorally during the marriage, they may have lost entitlement to receive maintenance, or may have been ordered to pay extra sums as a punishment.

Nowadays you will point out that fault plays a less prominent role. You could look at the law on divorce, financial orders and child disputes to give some examples of this. You could conclude your answer by thinking about why it is that fault no longer plays such an important role in family law. Is it because the courts (and society generally) are less certain about what is good and bad in moral terms? Or is it because the truth is that in many family cases both parties are equally at fault and there is little to choose between them. Finally, it might be argued that the courts have more important questions to focus on, such as what order will best promote the child's welfare.

> ✓ **Make your answer stand out**
>
> You might want to consider whether not making moral judgements is in fact a kind of moral judgement. Consider too the issue of child protection. Is that not an area where fault still plays an important role?

Glossary of terms

The glossary is divided into two parts: key definitions and other useful terms. The key definitions can be found within the chapter in which they occur as well as in the glossary below. These definitions are the essential terms that you must know and understand in order to prepare for an exam. The additional list of terms provides further definitions of useful terms and phrases that will also help you answer examination and coursework questions effectively. These terms are highlighted in the text as they occur but the definition can only be found here.

▓ Key definitions

Adultery	Adultery is voluntary sexual intercourse between a man and a woman, one or both of whom is married.
Cohabitants	Two persons who, although not married to each other, are living together as husband and wife or (if of the same sex) in an equivalent relationship.
Constructive trust	In order to establish a constructive trust, it is necessary to show: (1) a common intention to share ownership – this is proved by evidence of an express agreement to share ownership or it can be inferred from a direct contribution to the purchase price or mortgage instalment; (2) actions by the claimant in reliance on the common intention.
Consummation	Vaginal intercourse; the fact that contraception is used does not prevent there being consummation, but there must be penile penetration.
Female	The definition of female is that at birth the individual's genital, gonadal and chromosomal characteristics all pointed in the direction of being female.

Ground for divorce
The ground for divorce is that the marriage has broken down irretrievably, but that can only be proved by showing one of the 'five facts'.

Guardian *ad litem*
A court may appoint a guardian *ad litem* (often known just as a guardian) to represent the child's interests in court. The guardian should talk to the child and inform the court of the child's views.

Male
The definition of male is that at birth the individual's genital, gonadal and chromosomal characteristics all pointed in the direction of being male.

Molestation
Molestation includes acts that harass or threaten the victim. It must be conduct that is not simply an invasion of privacy.

No order principle
This is the principle in s. 1(5) of the Children Act 1989 that the court should only make an order if doing so would be better than not making an order at all.

Pension sharing order
This is an order that one party's pension be split at the time of the proceedings or thereafter. When the order comes into effect, the pension is split into two separate parts and they cease to be connected.

Placement
This is where the child lives with the would-be adopters for a form of 'trial' period to see if the adoption is likely to work.

Proportionality
Proportionality requires the degree of intervention into family life to be proportionate to the risk faced by the child. Further, it requires the courts to authorise an intervention to protect a child only if it is the least intrusive measure into family life that will adequately protect the child.

Proprietary estoppel
For X to be able to establish a proprietary estoppel, it must be shown that: (1) the owner of the property assured or promised X an interest in the property; (2) X relied on the promise to her detriment; (3) it would be unconscionable not to give X an interest in the property.

Resulting trust
A resulting trust is presumed to arise when A contributes to the purchase price of a piece of property that is put into B's name; or A transfers property to B, receiving nothing in return. In these cases it is presumed that B holds on trust for A.

Right
When a person has a right to *x*, other people are bound under a duty to protect or promote the interests the person has in *x*. There need to be good reasons why the person should be prevented from *x*.

Separation
Separation requires the parties to live in separate households.

| Special guardian | Special guardianship is designed to be more secure than merely giving someone a residence order, but not have the effect that an adoption has of ending the relationship between the child and birth family. |
| Surrogacy | Under a surrogacy arrangement, a couple ('the commissioning couple') ask a woman ('the surrogate mother') to carry a child for them. The agreement is that shortly after birth the surrogate mother will hand the child to the commissioning couple for them to bring up. |

■ Other useful terms

Acquired gender	The gender a person wishes to be recognised as having when applying under the Gender Recognition Act 2004.
Assisted reproduction	Medically assisted reproduction; it can involve the sperm and egg of the couple or donated gametes.
Autonomy	The right to be able to make decisions about how you wish to live your life.
Care plan	This is a document prepared by a local authority when applying for a care order; it will explain what the local authority intends to do while the child is in care.
Conscionability	This is the requirement of fairness.
Constructive desertion	Where one party is compelled to leave the other as a result of his or her bad behaviour.
Conveyance	This is the transfer of ownership of land from one person to another.
Duress	Threats or pressure exerted on someone to do something he or she does not really want to do.
Gender Recognition Certificate	This is the certificate issued under the Gender Recognition Act that confirms that for all legal purposes the person now has the gender stated in the certificate.
Genetic father	The man whose sperm led to the production of the child.
Jurisprudence	The philosophical basis of the law.
Legal aid	Government funding available to people in need to fund litigation and legal advice.
Licensed clinic	A clinic offering fertility treatment, which has been licensed under the Human Fertilisation and Embryology Act 1990.

Prohibited degrees of relationship

The Marriage Act 1949 lists those who are too closely related to be permitted to marry, those who are within the 'prohibited degrees of relationship'.

Special procedure

This is a name for the procedure dealing with undefended divorces, which means that the petitioner does not have to prove the facts alleged in the petition.

Index